To Mum and Dad
Gavin & Pearl Rendall

CONTENTS

ACKNOWLEDGMENTS

Special thanks to Nick Miller, keeper of Cavell memorabilia for St Mary's Church, Swardeston, Norfolk; the Imperial War Museum; the Royal London Hospital Archives and Museum; Pat Ashworth and Steve Fouch from CMF Nurses and Midwives; and Edith's biographers, Helen Judson, A. E. Clark-Kennedy, and Rowland Ryder who gathered first-hand recollections from the people who knew Edith Cavell personally, and who sought to sift the truth from the myths. Thanks to publisher Tony Collins for his encouragement, to Sheila Jacobs, Margaret Milton, and Jenny Ward for their attention to detail and helpful suggestions in the editing process, and to Adrian for his support and patience with his absentee wife, buried for months on end under books and notes about Edith.

FOREWORD

Christian faith and compassionate courage marked Edith Cavell's life. As Catherine Butcher shows in this timely book, Edith's life and motivation cannot be properly understood without reference to her faith.

There has been an explosion of interest in the First World War as we mark its centenary. This book reveals the personal story of a woman whose death made news around the world at the time. Edith's heroism and sacrifice resonated with her contemporaries. Catherine's well-researched biography now brings Edith Cavell to life for a new generation.

In the past century several books have been written about this remarkable woman, but few have sought to understand the statement which has become her epitaph, etched on her memorial statue near Trafalgar Square in London: 'Standing as I do in view of God and eternity, I realize that patriotism is not enough. I must have no hatred or bitterness towards any one.'

Catherine has traced the development of the faith and Christian commitment to forgiveness which undergird these words. As a vicar's daughter, Edith grew up reading the Bible and praying daily. That pattern continued throughout her school days, in her role as a governess, and as a nurse. Readers might not realize that prayers were a part of daily routine in hospital wards well into the twentieth century, and it is no surprise that Edith was seen praying at patients' bedsides. Sadly public prayers like these might cost contemporary nurses their jobs in many countries.

Like Edith, I trained at the London Hospital, where I appreciated the daily routine of prayers every morning, and I recognize the rigorous routine which Edith learned and passed on when she started the first nurses' training school in Belgium. She also put her faith into action caring for the poorest of the poor when she was nursing in England's infirmaries. In Belgium, once war broke out, she gave the same dedicated care to allies and enemies – even those who went on to betray her. Catherine shows how, even if Edith had not been executed, she deserves to be remembered.

This biography does not ignore Edith's critics. Her commitment to excellence, truth, and justice meant some saw her as 'strict'. But her high standards set a benchmark for the new Belgian hospitals. She did not shirk from truth-telling even when it put her own life in danger. She was prepared to die rather than risk one Allied soldier being captured and shot. Catherine also shows that Edith's faith was consistent: in her personal life she was loyal and caring – particularly towards her mother and the two young women she 'adopted' in Belgium.

As Catherine clearly portrays, it was Edith's faith that sustained her through ten weeks of solitary confinement. When the death sentence was pronounced she remained peaceful, confident in the certainty of 'The forgiveness of sins, the resurrection of the body, and the life everlasting', which she had affirmed daily in saying the Creed. We could learn much from Edith who used her last weeks in prison to reflect on her life and to make her peace with God and with those whom she knew. For Edith death was not the end.

And this testimony, written so thoughtfully and readably by Catherine, is proof that Edith's commitment to the Christian faith lives on – and can inspire and challenge us to consider how effectively we are putting our own faith into practice in our own lives in our own day.

The Baroness (Caroline) Cox

Abide with me: fast falls the eventide;
The darkness deepens; Lord, with me abide.
When other helpers fail and comforts flee,
Help of the helpless, O abide with me.

Swift to its close ebbs out life's little day;
Earth's joys grow dim, its glories pass away;
Change and decay in all around I see;
O Lord who changest not, abide with me.

I need thy presence every passing hour.
What but thy grace can foil the tempter's power?
Who, like thyself, my guide and stay can be?
Through cloud and sunshine, Lord, abide with me.

I fear no foe, with thee at hand to bless;
Ills have no weight, and tears no bitterness.
Where is death's sting? Where, grave, thy victory?
I triumph still, if thou abide with me.

Hold though thy cross before my closing eyes;
Shine through the gloom and point me to the skies.
Heaven's morning breaks, and earth's vain shadows flee;
In life, in death, O Lord, abide with me.

Henry Francis Lyte (1793–1847)

CHAPTER 1

EDITH'S FINAL HOURS

... TELL MY LOVED ONES LATER ON THAT MY SOUL, AS I BELIEVE,
IS SAFE, AND THAT I AM GLAD TO DIE FOR MY COUNTRY ...

(Edith Cavell, 12 October 1915)

The firing squad takes aim. In front of them, loosely tied to a post on the slope of a grassy field, a woman stands dressed in her nurse's uniform. Shots ring out through the mist of the autumn morning. Edith Cavell's body jerks forward. The nurse who had helped to save the lives of more than 200 Allied troops is dead. Dawn breaks.

Edith Cavell had confessed to the crime of 'conducting soldiers to the enemy' – soldiers who could potentially return to the battlefield. Guilty, she was sentenced to death by a German military court in occupied Belgium. Pleas for mercy fell on deaf ears. She went to her death calmly, confident that death is not the end.

That confidence came from her Christian faith and was confirmed in her final ten weeks of solitary confinement, as she reflected on her life and eternal destiny.

****

On 4 August 1915, a year after the United Kingdom declared war on Germany, Edith Cavell was arrested in Brussels for her role in the Belgian resistance movement. She was held in solitary confinement in St Gilles Prison in Brussels until a two-day trial on Thursday 7 and Friday 8 October. After a further weekend in solitary confinement, at 4.30 p.m. on Monday 11 October, sentence was passed: death at dawn by firing squad. Back in her cell, she spent her last evening on earth in prayer and contemplation.

Edith was a nurse who had seen many people die. She said she was not afraid of death. Now, as she faced the end of her own earthly life, she had a lifetime of rich inner resources to draw on to give her comfort and confidence alone in her tiny prison cell. She had spent her final weeks writing letters, reading her prayer book and the Thomas à Kempis classic *The Imitation of Christ*. Reflecting on her life, she prepared to meet her Maker.

She had been in England visiting her mother in the weeks before war was declared at the start of August 1914. Her mother wanted her to stay at home in England. Edith's response was: 'At a time like this I am more needed than ever.' Alerted to the imminent German invasion of Belgium, she returned to Brussels. By the time war was declared, she was ready to receive wounded soldiers into her pioneering nurses' training school on the outskirts of Brussels, which became a Red Cross hospital, caring for Allied and German casualties alike.

Thousands died within the first month of war. Wounded soldiers and those separated from their comrades found shelter with Belgians who were willing to risk their own lives to help Allied soldiers escape into neutral Holland. As Brussels fell to the invading army, Edith kept the nurses' training hospital running and it became a safe house for the fugitives. Working with the Belgian resistance movement, she helped more than 200 soldiers to safety. But spies were everywhere. It was only a matter of time before her clandestine operations were uncovered. Despite warnings, Edith couldn't stop. If she turned away an Allied soldier who was then caught and shot, it would be her fault, she said.

She knew that there were German spies among those who came to her for help. She knew the penalty for helping Allied troops to escape was death. She hoped that they would not execute a woman, but at the end, she was not fearful or full of hate. Her heart was filled with forgiveness, not bitterness. She went to her death confident that Jesus, her Lord, would be with her for her final journey through death and into his eternal presence.

The prison chaplain, a German Lutheran priest, Pastor Paul Le Seur, visited Edith in her cell when the death sentence had been passed. When he told her that the sentence would be carried out the next morning, Pastor Le Seur recalled, 'For one moment her cheeks were flushed and a moist film passed over her eyes – but only for a few seconds.'

He realized that as a German in uniform, she would find it difficult to gain spiritual support from him. Later he wrote:

> In addition, according to the principles of her Church,
> it was scarcely possible for her to receive the Sacrament
> from a pastor who did not belong to the Anglican
> Church, but I knew the Anglican chaplain in Brussels,
> the Rev. Gahan, very well, as a very pious Irishman,
> who, moreover, had been permitted to carry on his

religious duties without any trouble during the whole period of the occupation. I therefore asked Miss Cavell whether she wished that the Rev. Gahan should come to her to enable her to partake of the Holy Sacrament. Thereupon her eyes lighted up, and with great joy she accepted the proposal.

Revd Gahan led the church Edith attended in occupied Brussels. He had become a friend and was a guest at her last Christmas party.

Pastor Le Seur knew that it would be his duty to be with Edith at the last as she faced the firing squad on the execution site, the Tir National. Was this something she would like Revd Gahan to do instead? Caring for others as always, she refused.

'She declined this most definitely,' Pastor Le Seur recalled.

It would be much too heavy for Mr. Gahan, who was not accustomed to such things. 'Ah, Miss Cavell, I also am not accustomed to it,' I said, 'but shall I be rendering you a service if, instead of meeting you first outside on the Tir National, I come and fetch you here.' She accepted this offer gratefully. I said a few more words of Christian comfort to her from a deeply-moved heart, and then we parted from one another with a warm handshake.

Pastor Le Seur then went to Revd Gahan's house and left a note for him, as he was not at home. 'He was to come to me as soon as possible with his articles for Holy Communion.'

About 8 p.m. that evening, Revd Gahan went to visit Pastor

Le Seur: 'When I explained confidentially to him what was involved, he almost collapsed,' Le Seur recalled.

Revd Gahan then set off to the prison to share a final communion service with Edith. He wrote an account of their time together:

On Monday evening, October 11th, I was admitted by special passport from the German authorities to the prison of St. Gilles, where Miss Edith Cavell had been confined for ten weeks. The final sentence had been given early that afternoon.

To my astonishment and relief I found my friend perfectly calm and resigned. But this could not lessen the tenderness and intensity of feeling on either part during that last interview of almost an hour.

Her first words to me were upon a matter concerning herself personally, but the solemn asseveration which accompanied them was made expressedly in the light of God and eternity.

She then added that she wished all her friends to know that she willingly gave her life for her country, and said: 'I have no fear nor shrinking; I have seen death so often that it is not strange or fearful to me.'

She further said: 'I thank God for this ten weeks' quiet before the end.' 'Life has always been hurried and full of difficulty.' 'This time of rest has been a great mercy.' 'They have all been very kind to me here. But this I would say, standing as I do in view of God and eternity, I realize that patriotism is not enough. I must have no hatred or bitterness towards any one.'

Edith knew that people who had been close to her had played a part in her betrayal. Patriotism – her love of King and country – had brought her this far, but now she needed something more as she prepared to enter the kingdom of heaven. As a Christian, she had prayed daily, 'forgive us our trespasses, As we forgive them that trespass against us' and in saying the Creed as part of Morning Prayer, she had daily affirmed her belief in 'The Forgiveness of sins; The Resurrection of the body, And the life everlasting.'

Patriotism was not enough for these final hours. She knew that to enter into God's presence she needed to be forgiven. And just as Jesus' death had bought her forgiveness, she needed to forgive any and all who had wronged her.

Revd Gahan sat with Edith on her bed and they used the only chair in the cell as a table for Holy Communion. As they prepared to share bread and wine together, they said the Lord's Prayer, which Jesus taught his disciples; talking to God as 'Father'; longing for his kingdom to come; asking for daily provision and forgiveness 'as we forgive them that trespass against us'. Together they said the Creed, remembering that Jesus was crucified, buried, and on the third day he rose again from the dead. Then 'He ascended into heaven, And sitteth on the right hand of God the Father Almighty.'

The final words of the Creed had special relevance for Edith that evening: 'I believe in ... the Resurrection of the body, And the life everlasting.'

For Revd Gahan, the words he spoke as he gave Edith bread and wine also had a special poignancy.

The Body of our Lord Jesus Christ, which was given for thee, preserve thy body and soul unto everlasting life. Take and eat this in remembrance that Christ died for thee, and feed on him in thy heart by faith with thanksgiving.

The Blood of our Lord Jesus Christ, which was shed for thee, preserve thy body and soul unto everlasting life. Drink this in remembrance that Christ's blood was shed for thee, and be thankful.

As the communion service ended, Revd Gahan began to say the words of the hymn 'Abide With Me', and Edith joined him, repeating:

Abide with me: fast falls the eventide;
the darkness deepens; Lord, with me abide.
When other helpers fail and comforts flee,
Help of the helpless, O abide with me ...

Edith gave Revd Gahan the letters she had written to friends and family, and when they came to say goodbye, she smiled at him and said, 'We shall meet again.'

She was confident that death was not the end, and they would meet again in God's presence.

CHAPTER 2

GROWING UP IN THE VICARAGE

SOMEDAY, SOMEHOW, I AM GOING TO DO SOMETHING USEFUL. I DON'T KNOW WHAT IT WILL BE. I ONLY KNOW THAT IT WILL BE SOMETHING FOR PEOPLE.

(Edith Cavell, in a letter to her cousin Eddy)

Edith's confidence in the face of death didn't appear overnight. From the day she was born, that confidence was growing through thousands of different influences, spoken and unspoken, at home and in the wider world. Her Christian faith, which seems so remarkable to many in Britain today, was much more normal 100 years ago, and assured her that death is not the end for those who have put their trust in Jesus Christ.

Her father, Revd Frederick Cavell, was vicar of St Mary's parish church in Swardeston, Norfolk, for nearly half a century. One of five children, he grew up in London near St Pancras, and studied theology and philosophy in Heidelberg, Germany, a city he would later visit with his eldest daughter, Edith. He trained for ministry in the Church of England at King's College, London, and became curate of St Mark's Church, Islington in London.

This was where he met his wife, Louisa. Her widowed mother, Anna Warming, was a housekeeper. In Victorian times, she would have been described as 'a gentlewoman in reduced circumstances'. Her husband, Christian Abel Warming, had been a merchant seaman, master of one of the ships crossing the world. He was listed captaining a ship which arrived in Port Jackson, New South Wales, in August 1839. His fate is not clear, but by the time Anna and her daughter Louisa met Edith's father, Frederick, Anna was already widowed.

Louisa was Anna's second child, and the family were non-conformists, attending Wycliffe Chapel in London's East End, a congregation led by a noted philanthropist of the day, Revd Dr Andrew Reed. Wycliffe Chapel was one of the many churches that presented petitions for the abolition of slavery.

Louisa was christened at Wycliffe Chapel on 28 February 1836. She had at least four siblings, brothers Alfred, Henry and Rudolph and a sister, Christiana. Uncle Rudolph and Aunt Christiana both play a part in the family's story many years later. As a widow, Edith's grandmother was obliged to earn a living, a role which in due course brought Edith's mother, Louisa, and father, Frederick, together.

Coming from evangelical backgrounds with Puritan sympathies, Louisa and Frederick would have had a similar Christian zeal. Edith's mother, Louisa, was ten years younger than Frederick. He was seen to be serious and studious. Contemporaries described Louisa as charming and kind with a sweet personality and 'thoughtful consideration of others'.

To prepare his fiancée for life as a vicar's wife, Frederick paid for her to attend a finishing school. This training in the social graces included French, music, dancing, manners, and etiquette. Louisa would have learned to cook, clean, and run a household as well as learning to entertain. These were all skills which she would one day pass on to Edith and her sisters.

The couple married in 1864, and moved to the rural Norfolk village of Swardeston, where Frederick would become the vicar of St Mary's, a church dating back to Norman times. There was no vicarage. Their first home was a redbrick house with roses in the garden, but it was more than a quarter of a mile away from the church across the village common; not far, but not ideal.

When Frederick's father, a law stationer, died in 1863, as his father's third son Frederick inherited £1,000. This was a considerable sum in Victorian times, but Frederick was a man of Puritan principles and not inclined to spend money which he had not earned. Rather than keep the legacy to supplement his meagre parson's income, he used it to build a substantial vicarage for the parish on land next to the church, effectively giving away his inheritance. Generosity and self-sacrifice were values which characterized the Cavell family.

Edith was born on 4 December 1865, when the Cavells were still living in the temporary vicarage. Morning and evening prayers started and ended each day for the Cavell household. These excerpts from the Book of Common Prayer brought a rhythm to life. The same passage would be read on the same day every year, so we know the exact words Edith heard. The morning she was born, her father would have read from Isaiah 26:

> You will keep in perfect peace
> those whose minds are steadfast,
> because they trust in you. (v. 3)

Also

> As a pregnant woman about to give birth
> writhes and cries out in her pain,
> so were we in your presence, Lord. (v. 17)

And

> But your dead will live, Lord;
> their bodies will rise –
> let those who dwell in the dust
> wake up and shout for joy … (v. 19)

As a husband whose wife was about to give birth, Frederick might have perceived some special significance in the Bible readings. For Edith, the same vivid prophetic images were part of Morning Prayer on her birthday every year. As she grew to understand the words, these and many other verses from Scripture would begin to shape her faith.

The world into which Edith was born was changing fast. To put Edith's life into context, she was born the year Elizabeth Garrett Anderson became the first woman qualified in Britain to practise medicine. David Livingstone had just returned from exploring southern and central Africa, and was about to set off to find the source of the Nile.

Darwin's book *On the Origin of Species* had been published, prompting a hostile reaction on ideological, social, and religious grounds. Cartoonist Sir John Tenniel, reporting Disraeli's speech in Oxford in November 1864 captioned the cartoon: "'The question is,' Disraeli asked, "is man an ape or an angel? Now, I am on the side of the angels.'"

Explorers were the heroes of the age, and their reports to the Royal Geographical Society were major media events. Exploration also fuelled the Victorian missionary movement, and Christian values underpinned the philanthropy of the era.

In the late nineteenth century, science was the exploration of the natural world in all its aspects. Victorians loved to discover all things new, from flora and fauna to new countries and cultures. But science was not set in opposition to Christian faith; they were part of the same exploration. Many discoveries were made by men and women motivated by their zeal to explore God's creation and to spread the good news of the Christian gospel with words and actions.

In 1865, Hudson Taylor, who studied medicine at the Royal London Hospital in Whitechapel, London, had returned from mission work in China. He hosted the young Thomas John Barnardo at his house as a potential missionary candidate between 1865 and 1866. Thomas Barnardo went on to study at the London Hospital before becoming the founder and director of homes for poor children.

The Crimean War had ended a decade earlier in 1856, and Florence Nightingale had used her experience to lay the foundations for professional nursing by starting a nursing school at St Thomas' Hospital in London in 1860. A year later, she started a training school for midwives at King's College Hospital. Her book *Notes on Nursing*, completed in 1859, provided the basic curriculum at the Nightingale School and other nursing schools, such as the school in Brussels which Edith started in later life.

The high number of maternal deaths in the midwives' training school prompted the closure of Florence Nightingale's school for midwives. She went on to study maternal mortality and said,

> There is a large amount of preventable mortality in
> midwifery practice, and that, as a general rule, the
> mortality is far, far greater in lying-in hospitals than
> among women lying-in at home ... for every two
> women who would die if delivered at home, fifteen
> must die if delivered in hospital.

These findings were not published until 1871, but Edith was safely delivered at home in Swardeston's temporary vicarage.

Edith was baptized on 4 February 1866. The Heidelberg Catechism, which Revd Cavell would have ascribed to as an Anglican priest from the more Puritan wing of the church, says that the children of Christian parents 'belong to the covenant and people of God' and should be baptized 'to be ingrafted into the Christian Church'. Although Edith's mother had grown up in a non-conformist context, her Congregational Church upbringing would have also included infant baptism – promises made by parents on behalf of their child, then confirmed by the child in later life.

Using the words from the Book of Common Prayer, her parents promised to bring her up

> to lead a godly and a christian life ... to follow the
> example of our Saviour Christ, and to be made like unto
> him; that, as he died and rose again for us, so should
> we, who are baptized, die from sin, and rise again unto
> righteousness ...

As soon as Edith could read, she could see words of faith from former parishioners etched on the walls of the church and on the memorials she walked on in church as she went forward to receive a blessing at communion.

> Here rest in the hope of happy resurrection the remains
> ... of Elizabeth Aldrich ... and having attained to the
> age of LXXX years exchanged this life for immortality
> on the last day of December in the year of our Lord
> MDCLXXVIII.

> Here resteth the body of the virtuous and charitable
> Dorothy ... Who departed this life on the 29th day of
> September in the year of our Lord 1672 ... Waiting for
> ye glorious appearing of our Lord and Saviour Jesus
> Christ.

And,

> Mary, Wife of Isaac Marsh of Cambridge
> And daughter of John and Elizabeth Kemp of this Parish
> Who with pious resignation exchanged this life for a
> better
> On October 29th 1818
> In the 43rd year of her age
> She was an affectionate wife and tender mother

By all accounts, Frederick Cavell's strict and sombre Puritan lifestyle were complemented by his wife Louisa's kind and gentle nature. Revd Cavell would have used the evangelical mantra 'saved to serve' (see 2 Timothy 1:9). He was a man of considerable faith, but not an exception to the period.

The Christian faith was woven into the fabric of life in Britain in the second half of the nineteenth century. Although the 1851 census showed that 5 million people had not attended church the previous Sunday, the norm was for everyone to be part of a church or chapel. Bibles were available to read in railway stations. Often sermons were printed and sometimes became best-sellers. Christians were at the forefront of reform movements campaigning for the abolition of slavery, education for every child, votes for women, homes for fatherless children, and hospital care for the poor.

The Cavell family grew up knowing that all that they had was to be shared. Edith's sister Florence (known as Flor) was born in 1867, followed by Mary Lilian (known as Lil) in 1870, and John (known as Jack) in 1873. Being the vicar's children gave them some status. The 1870 Elementary Education Act made provision for all children to receive schooling from the age of five, but the Cavell children were taught at home by their parents rather than mixing with the village children. A governess would have been a costly addition to the household, for the limited income of a country vicar with no inheritance or rich benefactors to fall back on. It was not a rich parish. Records show that Edith's contemporaries, baptized in the same year as the vicar's daughter, included the children of a gardener, groom, farmer, carpenter, labourer, and blacksmith.

As mentioned above, each day in the Cavell household started and ended with daily prayers and Bible reading using the Book of Common Prayer. Morning Prayer included the Apostles' Creed with its firm affirmation: 'I believe in the ... Resurrection of the body, and the life everlasting.'

Sundays were special with Sunday school, church services morning and evening, a special Sunday lunch, and family prayers to end the day. Only religious books were allowed, and everyone dressed in 'Sunday best'. In her teens, Edith wrote to her favourite cousin, Eddy:

> I would love to have you visit us at Swardeston, but not
> on a Sunday. It's too dreadful, Sunday school, church
> services and family devotions morning and evening.
> Do come and stay again soon, but not for a weekend.
> Father's sermons are so long and dull.

Although they were not rich, the Cavell household included three servants. The staff were evidently paid a subsistence wage, as these words were scratched on an attic bedroom wall by a maid in 1876: 'The pay is small. The food is bad. I wonder why I don't go mad.'

Yet what the Cavells had, they shared. When the family were to enjoy a hot meal, the Cavell children were given covered bowls full of food to take to nearby parishioners. In later years, Edith told a friend that whenever roast meat was brought to the table, she felt the old fear that she wouldn't be able to enjoy it while it was still hot.

In this way the family learned to care for others and, as Revd Cavell was chaplain to the 100 inmates of the Henstead Union Workhouse at nearby Swainsthorpe, Edith grew up aware of the difficulties many faced. There was no state provision to fall back on, and each workhouse was run by a locally elected board of guardians. They employed the master and mistress who ran the workhouse, keeping paupers off the streets by providing board and lodging in return for hard work. Conditions were deliberately harsh, as Charles Dickens realistically portrayed in his novel *Oliver Twist*.

In one letter to her cousin Eddy, Edith wrote: 'Some day I am going to do something useful. It must be something for people. They are most of them so helpless, so hurt and so unhappy.'

His sermons may have been dull, but Frederick Cavell loved his children. Although he was strict, often he could be persuaded to put down his book to play. When the children pleaded: 'Pa, be a bear!' he got down on all fours to chase them through the house with fierce-sounding growls.

He taught Edith himself, and Frederick must have been close to his firstborn. When her father fell ill in later life, it was Edith who resigned from her job and returned home to nurse him, even though both her sisters had trained as nurses.

Norfolk had been one of the most prosperous counties in England before the Industrial Revolution. Acres of flat fields were ideal for farming. The wool trade flourished. Norfolk farmers pioneered new farming methods such as crop rotation in the early nineteenth century, and when industrialization meant other cities were becoming more prosperous, Norwich's railway station, opened in 1844, linked the county with the rapidly changing world beyond its borders.

When Edith was eight, Norfolk was the setting for one of the worst railway disasters in English history. A head-on collision at Thorpe station, Norwich, on 10 September 1874, left 100 people dead or injured. The noise of the collision was said to be like a great clap of thunder.

But life at the vicarage was protected from the turbulence of the Victorian world. Living in an agricultural community brings a rhythm to life. The seasons, which were reinforced by the church calendar, brought the Bible to life too. Lent, leading up to Easter, was a time to be frugal. Food stores from the previous harvest would be running low, and fasting helped to eke out meagre supplies.

Edith loved ice skating, and in freezing weather she would be found skating on Swardeston's ponds and the moat behind the church. As the winter frosts gave way to spring, ponds and streams thawed and soon every field, tree, and hedgerow was teaming with life: birds nesting, frogs spawning, and buds bursting open in every tree and hedgerow.

The countryside around Swardeston offered a paradise of wildflowers. More than 200 different species were found around the village, and Edith was fascinated by them.

In the summer there were long walks and games, dancing with her sisters around an old apple tree stump in the vicarage orchard, or running with hoops and sticks along the village roads.

Swardeston had a well-established cricket team, and long summer days meant cricket on the green. The new sport of Lawn Tennis was gaining popularity, and Wimbledon's first Ladies' Singles Tournament was played in 1884 when Edith was eighteen. She loved playing the game and often partnered a local champion.

Autumn days saw red squirrels gathering nuts in nearby woodland, and the Cavell children would also be found foraging for wild strawberries, blackberries, mushrooms, and rosehips. Jam-making parties were fun for all the family. The jam was then kept to be given to village families during the year.

Edith loved nature, and surrounded herself with plants and

animals. She painted flowers on a powder box as a gift for a new baby. Swardeston church has two of Edith's chalk drawings of reindeer dated October 1882 when she was sixteen. She gave her mother an album of pencil sketches of animals, leaves, flowers, and trees in the summer of 1886, and photographs of her in adult life show her with her favourite pets, two stray dogs which found a home with her in Brussels.

Like many other Victorian families, the Cavells spent time every summer on holiday by the seaside. The 1871 Bank Holidays Act established several days throughout the year as official holidays. Newly established railways sped holidaymakers to growing seaside resorts to eat ice cream or fish and chips, ride donkeys along the beach, watch Punch and Judy shows, and build castles in the sand. Revd and Mrs Cavell, together with their children, spent many holidays by the sea with their extended family, including cousin Eddy.

These holidays and carefree days in Swardeston gave Edith many happy memories, but when she reached fifteen her idyllic life changed significantly.

CHAPTER 3

PROMISES, PROMISES

O LET ME SEE THY FOOTPRINTS, AND IN THEM PLANT MINE OWN;
MY HOPE TO FOLLOW DULY IS IN THY STRENGTH ALONE.
O GUIDE ME, CALL ME, DRAW ME, UPHOLD ME TO THE END;
AND THEN IN HEAVEN RECEIVE ME, MY SAVIOUR AND MY FRIEND.

(The hymn Edith's mother inscribed in the confirmation Bible
she gave to Edith)

Edith's childhood furnished her with images of heaven: sunsets over Norfolk, fields full of flowers, family meals around the table, and lots of games and laughter. But her life changed considerably at the age of fifteen.

Edith's grandmother, Anna Warming, had gone to live in Margate with her daughter, Edith's aunt Christiana. Anna died on 28 March 1881 and, on 3 April 1881, the census records that Edith's mother, Louisa, was in Margate staying with her younger brother, Edith's uncle, Rudolph Warming, presumably to see her mother before she died. Christiana was named as executor of their mother's will.

In the busy run-up to Easter 1881, Revd Cavell remained in Swardeston with Edith, fifteen, Florence, thirteen, Mary Lilian, ten, Jack, eight, and the household's three servants: Harriet Baker, twenty-seven, described on the census form as a

34

'governess', Mary Pinnock, twenty-two, the cook, and Lavinia Pearce, twenty-one, the housemaid.

At fifteen, Edith would have been considered qualified to run the household with the servants, in her mother's absence. The age of consent was raised to thirteen in 1875 and then to sixteen in 1885. Queen Victoria's eldest daughter was engaged at fourteen and married at seventeen in 1855, and Edith's uncle John Cavell had married her aunt Caroline in 1861 when he was forty-one and Caroline was just seventeen.

However, her father had other plans, for at about this time, Edith was sent to school. The 1880 Elementary Education Act had made education compulsory until the age of ten. Although there was a village school in Swardeston, Edith's brother, Jack, was sent to school in Norwich, and Edith's first taste of education outside the vicarage was Norwich High School for Girls. She walked the four miles to school each day, dropping Jack off in the morning at Miss Brewer's school in Lime Tree Road, and collecting him after school before the walk home. The Cavells were keen on walking, so literally took the distance in their stride.

Over the next five years, Edith was to attend four different schools, first as a pupil, then as a pupil-teacher, eventually becoming a governess to a vicar's family in Essex. These changes could have been for a number of reasons, quite apart from Mrs Cavell's family responsibilities in Margate. Certainly her grandmother's estate of £50 14s might have helped towards school fees, which ranged from 1d to 3d a week for day schools at the time, and more for boarding schools.

An alternative reason for the changes in schooling could have been the fact that Edith was caught smoking in her father's study. Cigarettes had been manufactured in France since 1845 by the French state tobacco monopoly, and in the 1880s cigarette companies were mechanized, increasing output from thousands to millions of cigarettes every day. Ever one to explore boundaries, like her grandfather, the sailor Christian Abel Warming, Edith tried out the new craze for cigarette smoking. But by 1888, cigarettes were already being known colloquially as 'coffin nails'. Perhaps Revd Cavell decided Edith was picking up bad habits and needed a new educational environment. Certainly the servants recalled that he was in a thunderous mood for the whole day when he found his daughter smoking.

Norwich High School for Girls, the first Girls' Public Day School Company (GPDSC) school outside London, opened in February 1875 at the Assembly House in Theatre Street, Norwich. The GPDSC schools mixed girls of all classes and provided a high standard of academic education, with a definite remit to provide moral and religious education. This would have fitted Revd Cavell's requirements for his eldest daughter. School fees were deliberately kept low to allow a mix of pupils from all backgrounds. The first GPDSC school had opened at Chelsea in January 1873 and later transferred to Kensington – and was possibly where Edith was sent to boarding school for a short time. In later applications to train as a nurse, she said she went to school in Kensington.

Her third experience of school life was Belgrave School in Clevedon near Bristol. Family members could not give Edith's first biographers any reason why she should be sent to a school so far from home, but Rowland Ryder speculated:

Perhaps her father believed in travel broadening the mind and strengthening the independence; perhaps he thought it would be good for her to be away from her mother for a time – Mrs Cavell was inclined to be possessive where Edith was concerned.

While she was at school in Clevedon Edith was confirmed by the Bishop of Bath and Wells, Lord Arthur Hervey, on 15 March 1884.

Although Edith had been baptized as a baby, with her parents making promises to God on her behalf, she couldn't play a full part in the life of the church until she had been confirmed. Once she was confirmed, she could take Holy Communion, sharing the bread and wine to remember Jesus' broken body, his blood poured out on the cross, and his resurrection to new life. Up until she was confirmed, Edith would have approached the communion rail with her mother and the rest of the congregation. All those who had not been confirmed would receive a blessing, a short prayer asking for God's favour on her life by the presiding priest – usually her own father.

Before she could be confirmed, Edith would need to be able to say the Creed, the Lord's Prayer and the Ten Commandments by heart, as well as answering the questions on the Catechism. Learning by rote was the norm in Edith's time, and she'd have heard many of these words said most weeks on a Sunday.

The first two questions in the Catechism are: 'What is your name?' and 'Who gave you this name?' Having given her name, Edith would be expected to say: 'My Godfathers and Godmothers in my Baptism; wherein I was made a member of Christ, the child of God, and an inheritor of the kingdom of heaven.' Having repeated the promises made at her baptism, Edith would then have been asked: 'Dost thou not think that thou art bound to believe, and to do, as they have promised for thee?' Her answer:

> Yes verily; and by God's help so I will. And heartily
> thank our heavenly Father, that he hath called me to
> this state of salvation, through Jesus Christ our Saviour.
> And I pray unto God to give me his grace, that I may
> continue in the same unto my life's end.

Once again Edith was being reminded of her mortality, and the promise of eternal life for those who follow Jesus.

Edith would then have been asked to recite the Creed, with its strong statements about believing in 'God the Father Almighty, Maker of heaven and earth, and in Jesus Christ, his only Son our Lord ...'

The Creed describes Jesus after he has ascended into heaven, sitting at the right hand of God the Father, and concludes with a clear vision of followers of Jesus with new resurrection bodies and 'life everlasting'.

Having recited the Creed, Edith would also be expected to recite the Ten Commandments and to answer the question: 'What dost thou chiefly learn by these Commandments?' Edith's answer would have been: 'I learn two things: my duty towards God, and my duty towards my Neighbour.'

Having already seen her own father's strong sense of duty worked out in Swardeston, Edith would have had a clear idea of what this might mean as she said:

> My duty towards God is to believe in him, to fear him,
> and to love him, with all my heart, with all my mind,
> with all my soul, and with all my strength; to worship
> him, to give him thanks, to put my whole trust in him,
> to call upon him, to honour his holy Name and his
> Word, and to serve him truly all the days of my life.

Edith sought to remain true to this to the end. Although she was not remembered for talking publicly about her Christian faith, her actions put her faith into practice. Several contemporaries recall seeing her kneeling by her bedside praying, or praying with patients. She sought to show love to those around her. She honoured her parents and sought to care for them practically, and with regular letters to allay her mother's fears once she was in Belgium. She was loyal to the Queen, even when her employers made fun of Queen Victoria's prudishness. As she said in reciting the Catechism, she sought:

> To submit myself to all my governors, teachers,
> spiritual pastors and masters: To order myself lowly
> and reverently to all my betters: To hurt nobody by
> word nor deed: To be true and just in all my dealing:
> To bear no malice nor hatred in my heart: To keep my
> hands from picking and stealing, and my tongue from
> evil-speaking, lying, and slandering: To keep my body
> in temperance, soberness, and chastity: Not to covet
> nor desire other men's goods; but to learn and labour
> truly to get mine own living, and to do my duty in that
> state of life, unto which it shall please God to call me.

Once again, in these words from the confirmation service, there's the theme of duty and truthfulness. From all accounts of Edith's life, she sought to be true to this neighbourly duty.

A further part of confirmation preparation was to be able to recite the Lord's Prayer:

> Our Father which art in heaven, Hallowed be thy Name, Thy kingdom come, Thy will be done, in earth as it is in heaven. Give us this day our daily bread; And forgive us our trespasses, As we forgive them that trespass against us; And lead us not into temptation, But deliver us from evil. Amen.

Every confirmation candidate would be expected to know what this prayer was asking, and to explain it. Edith would have said the words set out in the Catechism as part of the *Daily Service-Book*:

> I desire my Lord God our heavenly Father, who is the giver of all goodness, to send his grace unto me, and to all people; that we may worship him, serve him, and obey him, as we ought to do. And I pray unto God, that he will send us all things that be needful both for our souls and bodies; and that he will be merciful unto us, and forgive us our sins; and that it will please him to save and defend us in all dangers ghostly and bodily; and that he will keep us from all sin and wickedness, and from our ghostly enemy, and from everlasting death. And this I trust he will do of his mercy and goodness, through our Lord Jesus Christ. And therefore I say, Amen, So be it.

The catechist would also be asked to explain the meaning of baptism and the 'supper of the Lord' – Holy Communion.

In preparing for confirmation in this way, Edith was reaffirming all she had been taught as a child in Norfolk. As an adult, Edith put her trust in Jesus – trust that continued throughout her life and gave her courage in the face of death.

The language of modern confirmation services is normally more contemporary than the words Edith would have said. Today a bishop asks all the candidates: 'Are you ready with your own mouth and from your own heart to affirm your faith in Jesus Christ?' Then the whole congregation is invited to welcome the candidates and 'uphold them in their life in Christ'. This emphasizes the importance of being part of a church, worshipping God together. Wherever Edith went she was part of the family of God, and even when the church she was part of in Belgium had to close when war broke out, she found another worshipping community of God's people. Their leader, Revd Stirling Gahan, was to be the last person to give her communion.

Confirmation takes place in the context of a communion service. The bishop addresses the candidates for confirmation: 'In baptism, God calls us out of darkness into his marvellous light. To follow Christ means dying to sin and rising to new life with him.'

Throughout the service there is an emphasis on turning away from evil and turning to Christ, submitting to him and coming to him as 'the way, the truth and the life'. The certainty of 'rising to new life' is emphasized.

The bishop's challenge to the confirmation candidates is:

Do not be ashamed to confess the faith of Christ
    crucified.
Fight valiantly as a disciple of Christ
against sin, the world and the devil,
and remain faithful to Christ to the end of your life.

The bishop's prayer for confirmation candidates such as Edith would have further emphasized the everlasting life of those who follow Jesus:

Almighty and everliving God ... Let thy fatherly hand,
we beseech thee, ever be over them; let thy Holy Spirit
ever be with them; and so lead them in the knowledge
and obedience of thy Word, that in the end they may
obtain everlasting life; through our Lord Jesus Christ ...

For her confirmation, Edith's mother wrote the following hymn in Edith's confirmation Bible. With its reference to life's end, and the glory of heaven, it has a prophetic quality for a daughter who was to reach the end of her life so dramatically:

O Jesus, I have promised to serve Thee to the end;
Be Thou forever near me, my Master and my friend;
I shall not fear the battle if Thou art by my side,
Nor wander from the pathway if Thou wilt be my Guide.

...

Oh, let me see Thy footprints, and in them plant
    mine own;
My hope to follow duly is in Thy strength alone.

Oh, guide me, call me, draw me, uphold me to the end;
And then in Heav'n receive me, my Savior and my
Friend.

The hymn, 'O Jesus I Have Promised', was written in 1868, by Revd John Ernest Bode for his daughter's and two sons' confirmation service. For Edith it was a prayer that underlined the importance of a Christian's duty and service and a reminder of her eternal destiny: 'That where Thou art in glory there shall Thy servant be.'

A month after Edith's confirmation, on 24 April 1884, her aunt, Christiana Warming, died in Margate. Her estate was £40. This might have prompted Edith's next move, this time to Peterborough; only eighty miles from her family home in Swardeston, compared to the 240-mile journey from Bristol.

She became a pupil-teacher at Laurel Court, Peterborough, a school for girls founded in 1870 by two friends, Miss Margaret Gibson and Miss Annette Van Dissel. The school, in the cathedral precincts, specialized in music, drawing, and languages, particularly Italian, French, and German. The fees were sixty guineas a year, paid in advance.

Irish-born Miss Gibson and Dutch-born Miss Van Dissel had met in Holland and travelled to England to start Laurel Court just after the Elementary Education Act of 1870 was passed. Between 1870 and 1880, 3,000 to 4,000 schools were started in England.

The fact that Miss Gibson went on to be made the first honorary free woman of Peterborough on her ninetieth birthday shows the high standing with which she was held. She was said to have the cathedral clergy under her thumb. She was sole principal when Miss Van Dissel returned to her native Holland, and she remained in post until her death in 1928 at the age of ninety-one, by which time she was blind.

Miss Gibson hated men and described them as 'Adamses'. When she received the freedom of the borough, her acceptance speech to the mayor ended with a typically eccentric comment:

> That person Adam never showed any chivalry to poor Eve. He was always looking and pointing to that fruit and what could she but do but sacrifice herself to the Adam whom I detest! Farewell and God bless you all!

Born in County Cork, like Edith, Miss Gibson was a clergyman's daughter. She wore a long black dress with a long train, a white knitted shawl and a muslin cap. To complete her almost cartoon-style caricature, she loved cats, which were free to roam the school, and her study was complete with 'an evil smelling wolf-skin rug' over the sofa.

Former pupils remember the school smelling of 'cats, margarine and treacle'. There was one indoor toilet for fifty people and baths once a week – 'but you were out of the bath almost before you were in'.

Miss Gibson 'knew what everyone was doing – or ought to be doing'. Her small stature contrasted with her large, forceful personality and her domineering character, which influenced every aspect of school life. Nothing could be done without her permission.

Her volatile temperament, quirky sense of humour, and self-confidence kept everyone on their toes. When she inspected the dormitories, anything that had been left out of place could be thrown out of the window by Miss Gibson. Discipline was strict, with Dickensian-style punishments: an offending girl could be locked in a cupboard or forced to sit cross-legged on the floor with a newspaper over her face.

The day started with breakfast at 6 a.m. and lessons at 7 a.m. for the boarders; day pupils arrived at 9 a.m. Prayers were part of every day, just as they had been for Edith at home in Norfolk. Girls were taken to the cathedral next door to Laurel Court forty-five minutes before the services started so they could read their prayer books. On Sundays they arrived at 10 a.m. and stayed until the end of the service, which finished at 12.30 p.m. In Lent and Advent they also spent Wednesday afternoons in the cathedral from 4 p.m. to 5.15 p.m., leaving before the evening service.

Miss Gibson's eagle eye and well-trained ear noticed if one of the girls put anything less than a penny into the church collection box. If she detected a lesser offering, at Sunday lunch she would say to the thirty or so gathered around the table: 'Young ladies, please, you are each expected to place a penny in the collection. No halfpennies please.'

Meals at Laurel Court were served in heavy silver dishes. Former pupils described the food as good, and on Miss Gibson's birthday there was always a birthday cake. Miss Gibson was particularly fond of soft bread and Bovril – originally known as 'Johnston's Fluid Beef' – it wasn't renamed until 1886.

Learning was by rote: memorizing pages from textbooks and writing answers to questions set by Miss Gibson on each subject. At certain points in the school day, pupils were not allowed to speak English; only French, German, or Italian was allowed. Au pair girls from the respective countries also helped with daily conversation practice so the pupils could become fluent speaking as well as reading other languages.

Piano practice was also mandatory, and at least one of the school's six pianos could be heard during most lessons as girls took turns to practise.

Edith was a pupil-teacher – the scheme had been started in Birmingham in the 1870s where pupil-teachers attended some classes to improve their own education, and helped with the teaching for the rest of their time. Edith was particularly good at French, and her aptitude was noticed by Miss Gibson, who later recommended her for her first post as a governess, and later for a post in Belgium.

And so Edith's education ended as it had begun: still in the shadow of the church, with days defined by morning and evening prayers, but now she was equipped to earn a living and motivated by a strong and capable headmistress, one of several strong role models who inspired Edith through her life.

CHAPTER 4

AN ETERNAL HOME

THERE YOU SHALL NOT SEE AGAIN ... SORROW, SICKNESS,
AFFLICTION, AND DEATH, FOR THE FORMER THINGS ARE PASSED
AWAY... IN THAT PLACE YOU MUST WEAR CROWNS OF GOLD ...
(John Bunyan's vision of heaven in *The Pilgrim's Progress*)

Edith returned to Swardeston after completing her education at Laurel Court. The village had changed very little in the time she had been away. *White's History, Gazetteer and Directory* from 1883 lists the occupations of the villagers: farmers, a cattle dealer, builders, market gardeners, a blacksmith, a butcher, a shopkeeper, shoemakers, a sub-postmaster, a schoolmaster, a sanitary inspector and rate collector, a victualler at the local pub, The Dog Inn, and the curate of Dunstone and Swainsthorpe, who also lived in the village.

Letters arrived every day at 7.20 a.m. and were dispatched via Norwich at 5.25 p.m. on weekdays and 10.40 a.m. on Sundays. The nearest telegraph office was in the village of Mulbarton, one and a half miles away.

Communication by telegraph was quite new. Queen Victoria had seen it used at the Great Exhibition in 1851, when she described it as 'the most wonderful thing ... Messages were sent out to Manchester, Edinburgh, &c., and answers received in a few seconds – truly marvellous!'

The Electric Telegraph Company, the world's first public telegraph company, was nationalized by the British government in 1870. But handwritten letters were still the normal method of communication. Charges for a telegram were several shillings compared with the standard penny post for any letter weighing under half an ounce to be sent from one part of the United Kingdom to any other part. When Edith was away from Swardeston, she wrote home regularly.

There were 339 inhabitants of the village, which had two manor houses; the Norman church with its four bells; a small Wesleyan chapel, built in 1840; the new vicarage, built by Revd Cavell in 1865; a school, built in 1877 for fifty pupils; and a mission room, built in 1880. As vicar, Edith's father received £180 a year, the use of the vicarage, the income from the glebe farm – land used to support a parish priest – and the income from tithes, which varied from parish to parish according to the numbers and income of local people.

Until 1836, parishioners gave a tenth of all they produced, such as corn, hay, fruit, cattle, or poultry – or a tenth of their wages – to support their vicar. But after the Tithe Commutation Act of 1836, tithes were no longer a legal requirement. One of Edith's tasks was to collect the eggs and butter from the glebe farm.

There was no Sunday school room for the parishioners to use and no money to build one. So, in the forthright manner Miss Gibson would have been proud of, without telling her parents, Edith wrote to the Bishop of Norwich, telling him about the need for a church room to house the growing Sunday school for the children of the village. The bishop replied that if the villagers could raise a proportion of the money needed, the diocese would fund the rest of the project.

The bishop might have thought he'd hear no more of it, but Edith set about raising the money. She had become a proficient watercolour painter, a skill encouraged as a pastime for the refined, well-educated lady. She had used her gift to decorate invitations to church events since childhood. Her uncle, John Cavell, was a professional artist, and gifted Victorian watercolourists such as Turner meant watercolour landscape painting was at the height of its popularity.

Edith's favourite artist is said to be Landseer, whose paintings of loyal dogs serving humanity were much loved by Victorians, particularly his paintings of rescue dogs. Landseer was the artist responsible for the bronze lions at the base of Nelson's Column. When he died in 1873, shops and houses in England lowered their blinds, flags flew at half-mast, and wreaths were hung around the lions' necks. He was buried in St Paul's Cathedral, London.

Although Edith was no Turner or Landseer, she put her artistic skills to good use. She set about her fundraising task by painting greetings cards. Since 1843 when Sir Henry Cole hired artist John Callcott Horsley to design a Christmas card that he could send to his friends and associates, greetings cards had been increasing in popularity as a method of communication. Developments in printing and the expanding postal service boosted the popularity of cards, and by the mid-1860s they were being mass-produced.

Edith's drawings of children in mop caps and pinafores resembled those of Kate Greenaway, a popular English children's book illustrator and watercolour artist, whose work was used by greetings card manufacturers.

The whole Cavell family joined Edith's enterprise to raise the money for the Sunday school room. Edith's father wrote a letter, enclosed with each of Edith's hand-painted cards, explaining the need for the room and asking for donations. Her mother addressed the envelopes, and her brother and sisters cut card, cleaned the paint boxes, and posted the cards to everyone in the parish and further afield.

Edith's determination and perseverance paid off. Within a year, their efforts raised the substantial sum of £300 for the Sunday school room, and the bishop kept his side of the bargain. The single-storey room was built next to the vicarage and opened in 1888.

Even before the new room was built, both Mrs Cavell and Edith taught in the Sunday school which met in a local rented house. Edith and her mother were both godmothers to a number of local babies, giving them signed copies of the Bible and *The Pilgrim's Progress* as gifts.

John Bunyan's *The Pilgrim's Progress* was a book considered suitable for Sunday reading when many other pastimes were restricted by strict Victorian sabbath observance rules. Edith would have known *The Pilgrim's Progress* well, and its images of heaven would have been the pictures in her mind as she thought about her eternal destiny.

The two-part allegory of Christian and Christiana on the journey from their home in the City of Destruction to the Celestial City, provides a vision of heaven and also strong female role models in the characters of Christiana, Prudence, Piety, Charity, and Mercy.

The characters are vividly described, and the illustrated versions published in Victorian times brought the story to life for the Cavell children, with maps and pictures showing the characters in action.

. The place-names Bunyan created paint their own metaphorical pictures. The plot moves quickly from the City of Destruction to the Slough of Despond, the Wicket Gate, the Hill Difficulty, and House Beautiful; through the Valley of Humiliation and the Valley of the Shadow of Death, to Vanity Fair; then on past the River of the Water of Life, By-Path Meadow, to Doubting Castle, the home of Giant Despair; and finally to the Delectable Mountains, the Enchanted Ground, the Land of Beulah, through the River of Death, to the Celestial City.

This allegorical journey and the Bible references throughout it would have given Edith a graphic illustration of how God works through the ups and downs of a person's life.

Passages from *The Pilgrim's Progress* describing heaven would have been in Edith's mind as she prepared for her own journey through 'the River of Death' to the 'Celestial City'. In later life she wrote wistfully to her cousin Eddy about their childhood days 'when we were young and life was fresh and beautiful and the country so desirable and sweet'. She could also have had in mind Bunyan's description of the River of the Water of Life, with its 'green trees, that bore all manner of fruit' and the meadow that was 'curiously beautified with lilies ... green all the year long'. These images, taken from Psalm 23:2 and Isaiah 14:30, were also descriptions of the orchards and fields around her Norfolk home.

Bunyan's allegory gave his Victorian readers images to make sense of life's difficulties, and hope that death is not the end.

The Victorians were obsessed with death, particularly after Prince Albert's death in 1861, when Queen Victoria went into mourning, wearing black for the next forty years.

By 1900 in Britain, when Edith turned thirty-five, life expectancy averaged forty-seven for a man and about fifty for a woman – but 33 per cent of deaths were of the under-fives. Death was a familiar occurrence, and Victorian children were not spared the details. Their approved Sunday reading included Bunyan's description of Faithful's martyrdom:

> They therefore brought him out, to do with him
> according to their law; and, first, they scourged him,
> then they buffeted him, then they lanced his flesh with
> knives; after that, they stoned him with stones, then
> pricked him with their swords; and, last of all, they
> burned him to ashes at the stake. Thus came Faithful to
> his end.

But this brutal martyrdom also came with a promise of an eternal future. Bunyan wrote:

> Now I saw that there stood behind the multitude a
> chariot and a couple of horses, waiting for Faithful, who
> (so soon as his adversaries had despatched him) was
> taken up into it, and straightway was carried up through
> the clouds, with sound of trumpet, the nearest way to
> the Celestial Gate.

Heaven and hell were vivid and real in Victorian England. Bunyan also made it clear to his readers what it meant to be a follower of Jesus. Hopeful, Christian's companion on the journey, says:

> One day I was very sad, I think sadder than at any
> one time in my life, and this sadness was through a
> fresh sight of the greatness and vileness of my sins.
> And as I was then looking for nothing but hell, and
> the everlasting damnation of my soul, suddenly, as I
> thought, I saw the Lord Jesus Christ look down from
> heaven upon me, and saying, 'Believe on the Lord Jesus
> Christ, and thou shalt be saved.' [Acts 16:30–31, KJV]
>
> But I replied, Lord, I am a great, a very great sinner.
> And he answered, 'My grace is sufficient for thee.' [2
> Corinthians 12:9, KJV] ...
>
> And I heard him say, 'And him that cometh to me, I
> will in no wise cast out.' [John 6:37, KJV]

Bunyan's character, Hopeful, said that Jesus Christ 'made me love a holy life, and long to do something for the honour and glory of the name of the Lord Jesus...'

That commitment to honour and serve Jesus, dedicating her life to others, was something Edith shared. She saw the unhappiness of so many people around her and wanted to make life better for them.

Later, as a nurse in England or in Belgium, Edith was often surrounded by misfortune and death. The view Bunyan described of the Celestial City would have given Edith her own vision of heaven:

> It was builded of pearls and precious stones, also the
> street thereof was paved with gold ... [there were]
> orchards, vineyards, and gardens, and their gates
> opened into the highway ...

> ... the reflection of the sun upon the city (for the
> city was pure gold) was so extremely glorious that they
> could not, as yet, with open face behold it ...

After Bunyan's characters Christian and Hopeful see the Celestial City, they realize that they have still to cross a river – the River of Death:

> ... but there was no bridge to go over: the river was very
> deep.

Christian is full of doubt and is aware of his own shortcomings, but Hopeful is full of faith. In the allegory, this means that Christian finds the water deep, and he begins to sink. Crying out to his friend, Hopeful, he says: 'I sink in deep waters; the billows go over my head, all his waves go over me!'

In contrast, Hopeful can feel the bottom of the river.

In years to come, Edith would approach her own death with confidence, trusting that, like Hopeful, she would be able to say: 'I see the gate, and men standing by to receive us.'

As Hopeful reminds Christian in Bunyan's allegory:

> These troubles and distresses that you go through
> in these waters are no sign that God hath forsaken
> you; but are sent to try you, whether you will call to
> mind that which heretofore you have received of his
> goodness, and live upon him in your distresses.

Like Christian, Edith would draw on the words of Isaiah 43:2: 'When thou passest through the waters, I will be with thee, and through the rivers, they shall not overflow thee' (KJV).

And with that confidence, Christian and Hopeful both passed through the River of Death leaving their 'mortal garments behind them in the river'.

The vision Edith had of heaven was informed by Bunyan's dream: '… the beauty and glory of it was inexpressible'.

Here's how the angelic beings in Bunyan's dream describe it:

> There, said they, is the Mount Zion, the heavenly Jerusalem, the innumerable company of angels, and the spirits of just men made perfect. [See Hebrews 12:22–24.] You are going now, said they, to the paradise of God, wherein you shall see the tree of life, and eat of the never-fading fruits thereof; and when you come there, you shall have white robes given you, and your walk and talk shall be every day with the King, even all the days of eternity. [See Revelation 2:7; 3:4; 21:4,5.]

Edith was taught that in the beauty and perfection of heaven with God, the King of kings, there was no sadness, illness or tears. It was this confidence that enabled Victorians to be positive in the face of death. Death was familiar territory but eternity was full of joy. As Bunyan said:

> There you shall not see again … sorrow, sickness, affliction, and death, for the former things are passed away… In that place you must wear crowns of gold … There you shall enjoy your friends again that are gone thither before you; and there you shall with joy receive … There also shall you be clothed with glory and majesty …

Bunyan describes a heavenly welcome for Christian and Hopeful as they approach the gates of heaven:

> Now while they were thus drawing towards the gate,
> behold a company of the heavenly host came out
> to meet them ... that they may go in and look their
> Redeemer in the face with joy. Then the heavenly host
> gave a great shout, saying, 'Blessed are they which
> are called unto the marriage supper of the Lamb.'
> [Revelation 19:9, KJV]

At the end of her life, as she stood before the firing squad, this vision of heaven would have been what Edith anticipated was waiting for her.

> There came out also at this time to meet them several
> of the King's trumpeters, clothed in white and shining
> raiment, who, with melodious noises, and loud, made
> even the heavens to echo with their sound. These
> trumpeters saluted Christian and his fellow with ten
> thousand welcomes from the world; and this they did
> with shouting, and sound of trumpet ... But, above
> all, the warm and joyful thoughts that they had about
> their own dwelling there, with such company, and that
> for ever and ever. Oh, by what tongue or pen can their
> glorious joy be expressed! And thus they came up to
> the gate ...

This vision of a warm welcome, joy, and an eternal home gave Edith and other Victorians an enduring hope that, although this life might be full of trouble, it is short and in complete contrast with the glorious and eternal life to come.

Bunyan continues:

> Now I saw in my dream that these two men went in at
> the gate: and lo, as they entered, they were transfigured,
> and they had raiment put on that shone like gold. There
> was also that met them with harps and crowns, and gave
> them to them the harps to praise withal, and the crowns
> in token of honour.
>
> Then I heard in my dream that all the bells in the
> city rang again for joy, and that it was said unto them,
> 'ENTER YE INTO THE JOY OF YOUR LORD.' I
> also heard the men themselves, that they sang with
> a loud voice, saying, 'BLESSING, AND HONOUR,
> AND GLORY, AND POWER, BE UNTO HIM THAT
> SITTETH UPON THE THRONE, AND UNTO THE
> LAMB, FOR EVER AND EVER.' [Revelation 5:13, KJV]
>
> Now, just as the gates were opened to let in the men,
> I looked in after them, and, behold, the City shone like
> the sun; the streets also were paved with gold, and in
> them walked many men, with crowns on their heads,
> palms in their hands, and golden harps to sing praises
> withal.
>
> There were also of them that had wings, and they
> answered one another without intermission, saying,
> 'Holy, holy, holy is the Lord.' [See Revelation 4:8.] And
> after that they shut up the gates; which, when I had seen
> … I wished myself among them.

As a nurse, Edith saw death often. When the time came to prepare for her own death, these images of heaven, together with a lifetime of Scriptures and other encouragement, gave her confidence to remain unflinching in the face of the firing squad.

CHAPTER 5

VALUES TO LIVE BY

MISS CAVELL JUST LAUGHED AT OUR ANTICS. SHE WAS FULL OF
FUN, AND LIKED TO SEE US HAPPY TOGETHER ... [THERE WAS]
ALWAYS A SMILE ON HER FACE.

(Jack Powell, whose childhood governess was Edith Cavell)

At the end of 1886, Edith turned twenty-one. She was five foot three inches, slight in build, with brown hair and grey eyes. While her wealthier contemporaries might have been attending 'coming out' parties and preparing for marriage, Edith had to find work. With a recommendation from Miss Gibson at Laurel Court, she took up her first role as a governess in Steeple Bumpstead in Essex. Edith's task was to look after the vicar's children. Before becoming vicar of Steeple Bumpstead, Revd Charles Mears Powell had been vicar of All Souls, Langham Place – a London church which has become well known worldwide for its evangelical Bible teaching.

Kathleen, eleven, Constance, nine, Mabel, eight, and Jack, six: the four Powell children remembered Edith as being 'great fun' although she was strict. As their mother was an invalid, Edith was responsible for their care and education as well as many of the duties normally reserved for the vicar's wife, such as entertaining visitors and arranging the church flowers.

The village was preparing for Queen Victoria's Golden Jubilee, to be celebrated on 20 and 21 June 1887. Organizing stalls for church functions was one of Edith's many roles, which she would have completed with her usual enterprise and efficiency.

Life was very similar to life at the vicarage in Swardeston, with its rhythm of daily family prayer and worship. The older children were expected to study the Book of Common Prayer as Edith had done at Laurel Court. She would have taught each of the Powell children the Catechism with its questions and answers on 'salvation through Jesus Christ', the articles of faith, the Ten Commandments, the Lord's Prayer and the sacraments of baptism and Holy Communion. As well as the Book of Common Prayer, the Bible, and *The Pilgrim's Progress*, Edith may well have followed the suggestion of the newly formed Mothers' Union on other suitable religious books to read to children, such as *The Peep of Day: A Series of the Earliest Religious Instruction the Infant Mind is Capable of Receiving*, which gives an insight into Victorian Christian teaching aimed at children.

The Peep of Day was a lighter read than the Book of Common Prayer, as it focused on Bible stories starting with simply worded basics:

> My dear little children; – You have seen the sun in the sky.
> Who put the sun in the sky? – God.
> Can you reach up so high? – No.
> Who holds up the sun that it does not fall? – It is God.

God lives in heaven; heaven is much higher than the sun.
Can you see God? – No.
Yet He can see you, for God sees everything.

The book didn't shirk from a typical Victorian emphasis on death, with rhymes such as:

My little body's made by God
Of soft warm flesh and crimson blood;
The slender bones are placed within,
And over all is laid the skin.

My little body's very weak;
A fall or blow my bones might break;
The water soon might stop my breath;
And fire might close my eyes in death.

But God can keep me by His care;
To Him I'll say this little pray'r:
'O God from harm my body keep
Both when I wake and when I sleep.'

The Peep of Day also addressed the difficult concept of the soul: 'Your body can die, but your soul cannot die. What is your soul made of? Your soul, or spirit, is made of the breath of God. When your body dies, your soul will be alive, and you will not be quite gone. Even a baby has a soul, or a spirit.'

In this black and white world of good and evil, everything related to the life of faith and the future assurance of heaven. Even the description of a whale in *The Peep of Day* took on a religious dimension: 'It is a fish as long as a church.'

In the world Edith inhabited, heaven was a definite destination. As *The Peep of Day* explained: 'You know, my little children, we are wicked, and God can make us good with His Holy Spirit. If God puts His Holy Spirit in us, we shall love Him and live with Him in heaven.'

In explaining the way to heaven, *The Peep of Day* described the conversation between the thief 'who was sorry for his sins' who said to Jesus from his cross at the crucifixion, 'Remember me when you come to be King.'

The Peep of Day continues:

> Jesus said, 'You shall be with me in heaven today.' So Christ heard the poor thief's prayer; for Jesus died that He might save all who believed that He was the Son of God. If you go to heaven you will see the poor thief.

Teaching the children about their Christian faith would be part of Edith's role, as well as teaching them English, French, and piano. The popular hymns of the day were also a source of Christian teaching and would have been part of Edith's repertoire on the piano as well as in church.

For the Powell children in Edith's care, life wasn't all school work and church attendance as it had been for Edith at Laurel Court. She took the children to play ball games on the village recreation ground. Jack learned to play cricket and became a keen cricketer. A contemporary told one of Edith's biographers, Rowland Ryder:

> My brother and I had a goat and little go-cart which we used to ride up and down the meadow while Miss

Cavell just laughed at our antics. She was full of fun,
and liked to see us happy together … [There was]
always a smile on her face.

Edith also loved dancing, and about this time, she bought some
new shoes for a dance she wanted to attend. However, she was
prone to chilblains and when the day came she was suffering
badly, but went dancing anyway. She said later: 'I danced and
danced until my feet bled and the new shoes I had bought
especially for the occasion were completely spoilt – but I found
that my chilblains had gone!'

Each summer the Powell family spent a month by the sea, as
the Cavell family had done in Edith's own childhood. Clacton-
on-Sea, forty-five miles away from Steeple Bumpstead, was
the resort they chose, with lots of space for picnics and games
on the long sandy beach. Steamships run by the Woolwich
Steam Packet Company docked on Clacton Pier, which was
just 160 yards long; it was more than doubled in length to 393
yards in 1893 when Clacton became a popular destination for
day-trippers.

Edith kept in touch with her own family just seventy miles
away in Swardeston. Her uncle George, one of her father's older
brothers and a former stockbroker, had died in December 1886
leaving a substantial estate of £18,235. Probate was granted the
following summer, and a legacy from his estate might have
been what prompted the Cavell family to visit Germany and
Austria the following year. Edith and her brother Jack travelled
with Revd and Mrs Cavell and Edith's friend Alice Burne, who
kept a diary.

Edith and Alice went ahead of the family by train to visit Frankfurt: Frankfurt Central Station had been newly opened that year. There they visited the Palmengarten, the largest botanical garden in Germany, opened to the public in 1871, with its climatized greenhouses containing collections of plants from around the world.

From Frankfurt they went on to visit Heidelberg, where Revd Cavell had been a student, before spending a month at St Goar, named after Goar of Aquitaine, a seventh-century monk who became known for his generous hospitality.

As well as swimming, tennis, and sightseeing, Edith took the opportunity to practise her French and to learn some German. Around this time she visited a free hospital run by a Dr Wolfenberg, and was so impressed that she set up a fund for the hospital to buy surgical instruments. Like her father, she was eager to give to the poor, and it would seem that her interest in medicine was starting to grow.

But back home in England, the Powell children were becoming too old for a governess, so her work for the family came to an end. Soft-hearted Edith and the children were all in tears as she said goodbye.

Three more posts as a governess to different affluent families then followed: the four Gurney children at Keswick New Hall in a village very near Swardeston, the two Barclay children at Colney Hall five miles away, and the three Pryor children, eighty miles away near Chelmsford in Essex. Meg Gurney remembered Edith for her gentleness, although the Pryor children recalled her as serious and apparently unhappy.

When her work with the Pryors came to an end, Mrs Pryor's parting gift to Edith was a copy of the classic devotional book by the fifteenth-century German priest, Thomas à Kempis. This small book, *The Imitation of Christ*, was much used by Edith, who memorized quotations and highlighted several key passages, especially during her last weeks while in solitary confinement before her execution.

Perhaps the change from someone 'full of fun' to a more sombre state was caused by disappointed love. Edith and her second cousin Eddy had been close friends since early childhood. Had he proposed, it is said that Edith is likely to have accepted. But Eddy had inherited a nervous condition from his mother and thought he ought not to marry, though Edith and Eddy remained friends and corresponded throughout her life. On the day of her execution, Edith wrote a dedication to Eddy on her copy of *The Imitation of Christ*, leaving him one of her last and most treasured possessions with the words: 'With love to E. D. Cavell'.

Paul François, a wealthy lawyer in Brussels, was her next employer; once again she was appointed on the recommendation of Miss Gibson of Laurel Court. There were four children: Marguerite, thirteen, Georges, twelve, Hélène, eight, and Evelyn, three. The family lived in an affluent avenue in Brussels but also owned stables, a yacht, and a country chateau near the Dutch border.

Edith was employed to care for the children, teaching them herself until they were old enough for her to take them to school. She was also responsible for their meals, clothes, leisure activities, and spiritual nurture, including taking them to church and reading to them. She chose the popular children's novels of the day; tales with Christian morality and values woven through the stories, such as *Little Women* by Louisa May Alcott and *Little Lord Fauntleroy* by Frances Hodgson Burnett. At the time, Burnett's more popular book *The Secret Garden* had not yet been written. She also introduced them to her favourite writers: Charles Dickens, and the poets Longfellow, Wordsworth, and Tennyson, with poems such as Longfellow's 'Psalm of Life' which expressed Edith's determination to make a difference; to leave 'footprints on the sands of time'.

Edith was employed to speak to the François children in English, although she spoke French to their parents. As well as more conventional lessons, she used games to teach skills such as laying the table, cooking, and painting the scenery for plays performed for the children's parents. In one game she encouraged the children to write questions and answers for each other. In answer to the question: 'What is your greatest ambition?' Edith wrote: 'To be buried in Westminster Abbey.' She might simply have been using the game to expand the children's vocabulary, rather than to reveal her own hopes and dreams. However, the words she wrote seem somewhat prophetic with hindsight. Although she was not buried in Westminster Abbey, there was a memorial service held for Edith at the abbey as the coffin carrying her home to Norfolk passed through London.

As part of the same children's game, Edith revealed that her favourite book was *Robert Elsmere* written by Mrs Humphry Ward in 1888. The story is a romance between Robert Elsmere, a young Anglican clergyman, and Catherine Leyburn, who is dedicated to her family and known for her seriousness and spirituality. Robert persuades her to marry him, promising her that their life together will be devoted to God and to helping others. Perhaps Edith identified with the social conscience and serious, spiritual character of the heroine.

A common thread in several of her favourite literary works is strong, spiritual women with a sense of purpose, and heroes with Christ-like virtues who cared for the poor, the sick, and the uneducated.

Although Edith was a Protestant living in a Catholic home, the children remembered her as being tolerant and careful to ensure that they learned their own Catholic traditions. While she was employed by the François family, it is said that she attended the Chapelle de la Résurrection, a Catholic church with an ecumenical emphasis, about thirty minutes' walk from the François's home in the Avenue Louise. The church is still in Brussels and describes itself as 'a home for everyone' ... 'a Chapel for Europe'.

In later life, Hélène and Evelyn told author A. E. Clark-Kennedy, one of Edith Cavell's biographers, that Edith was strict but always fair. If she did have to discipline them, she always explained why. She led by example, was always ready to do whatever she asked of the children, and believed that healthy children should be prepared to withstand all weathers. She rarely allowed them to travel by tram, instead taking them on long walks, as well as walking to and from school.

She was strict about telling the truth too. One, possibly apocryphal, story, suggests that when Mme François asked her to tell any callers that she was out, Edith refused. She would not tell a lie.

The François sisters also remembered Edith's patriotism. At dinner one evening, her employer criticized Queen Victoria for her Puritanical ways. Edith stood up and announced:

'Monsieur, I can listen to no criticism of my Queen!' and promptly left the room.

During her five years with the François family, Edith continued to paint, and a few of her watercolours from this period have survived. She taught the children to draw and paint too, to collect and name wildflowers, and to care for the family pets – especially the dogs. She wrote and illustrated a small booklet on how to care for dogs; how to prepare dog food, how dogs should be groomed, and how to make a kennel. In it she wrote: 'A dog soon reciprocates little kindnesses and instinctively takes upon himself the duty of protector.' Later, when Edith was taking fugitive Allied soldiers to rendezvous with other members of the Belgian resistance movement, her faithful dog Jack was frequently at her side, protecting his mistress.

Edith's prizes for her pupils were often her own small pen and ink drawings or watercolours, which included sketches of roses and of the family's summer home in the Belgian countryside. Her black and white illustrations also decorated the family's dinner party menus. One elaborate dinner party included twelve courses, such was the opulence of the François family lifestyle.

It would have been easy to enjoy this affluent and comfortable existence throughout her career, but Edith saw the role of governess as 'only temporary'. As she wrote to her cousin Eddy: 'Someday, somehow, I am going to do something useful. I don't know what it will be. I only know that it will be something for people. They are, most of them, so helpless, so hurt and so unhappy.'

Her summer breaks were spent in Swardeston, playing hockey, tennis, and games with the family. She was a particularly good tennis player, but entered enthusiastically into any games. Writing in later life, Helen Swann, a family friend, remembered a visit to the Cavell family in 1892, when she was nine and Edith was twenty-six:

> The whole family was there, all of us of the younger generation – the three Cavell girls, their brother Jack, my sister, her friend and I. We went into the study after tea, and settled down to play a very noisy game called 'Animal Grab'. I sat next to Edith, and was thrilled because she made a fuss of me, as I recovered from some childish ailment. Edith, I remember, was a lion and I was a mouse. I got frightfully excited, and made a tremendous noise. In fact Mr and Mrs Cavell came into the study to see what it was all about. Edith was much amused at my excitement. 'Well, Helen,' she said, as we made our departure, 'you were really very unlike a mouse.'

But not everyone remembered Edith as fun-loving and carefree. William Alfred Towler, the postmaster at Swardeston, told biographer Clark-Kennedy he remembered her as over-serious and, even in her twenties, she seemed to be driven by an inner sense of purpose.

In 1895, her father was taken ill. Both her sisters were already working away from home as nurses, so Edith resigned her post in Brussels to return home to care for him. Tears were shed as she said goodbye to the François family after five years as their governess. She returned to her roots in Norfolk, resumed Sunday school teaching, and also played the harmonium for church services. The modern hymns of the time such as 'Blessed Assurance' and 'All the Way my Savior Leads Me', by the prolific hymn writer Fanny Crosby, gave assurance of God's guidance and care throughout life.

Music in Swardeston's parish church was one of Edith's concerns. One of the choir boys at Swardeston, Frederick Davey, wrote in his memoirs that he took milk and eggs from the glebe farm to the Cavell family once or twice a week.

> When it was flower time I used to gather a bunch to give to my Sunday school teacher, Miss Edith … O the joy it gave me to make some excuse to go to the Rectory with some little thing, in order to get one of her smiles and a few kind words.

Edith noticed that he could sing well and suggested that he joined the church choir. He declined, saying, 'To tell you the truth, Miss Cavell, when I'm lying in bed I've only got one spare suit!' He didn't feel able to attend church without a 'Sunday best' suit. Edith laughed and said, 'We mustn't let a thing like that stop us, Freddie! We'll see what we can do!'

She found one of her brother's old suits and gave it to Freddie, who then joined the choir. It was a turning point for the boy, who described himself as a 'street Arab'. When he was eleven, he had run away from home, and was working for a local farmer. With his new-found self-respect – and Jack's suit – he left Swardeston, married, and settled in Lowestoft where he and his wife brought up their daughter.

Edith had helped a young man discover his potential. And the months back home, caring for her father, seem to have helped her clarify her own future. She had invested ten years of her life in caring for children, teaching them her values as well as providing them with an education. Much of that time had been in the comfort of affluent homes with prosperous families. She had travelled through Europe, learned to speak French fluently, and had found what Jane Austen would have described as 'resources for solitude' in reading, sketching, and in her Christian faith.

At the end of 1895 Edith turned thirty; evening prayers at home with her mother and father on 4 December included reading John's Gospel chapter 13, with Jesus' exhortation: 'A new command I give you: love one another. As I have loved you, so you must love one another. By this everyone will know that you are my disciples, if you love one another' (John 13:34–35) followed by Peter's boastful blustering: 'Lord ... I will lay down my life for you' (verse 37).

Two days later, Edith was ready to set aside the safety and comforts of home to take on a physically exhausting role that would put her own health at risk. She applied to become Assistant Nurse, Class II, at the Fountain Fever Hospital in Tooting.

CHAPTER 6

A NEW CAREER IN NURSING

TRY AND FIND SOMETHING USEFUL TO DO, SOMETHING TO MAKE
YOU FORGET YOURSELF WHILE MAKING OTHERS HAPPY.

(Edith Cavell, in a letter written on the day before she died to her
ward, Grace)

Just six days after her application to the Fountain Fever
Hospital, Edith started work as a nurse on 12 December 1895.

The hospital in Tooting had been built hurriedly in just nine
weeks in 1893 to cope with an outbreak of scarlet fever. The
eight rows of temporary wooden huts, arranged across a central
block, could accommodate 400 patients as well as the nursing
and domestic staff.

Truthful and blunt as ever, Edith's application form stated:
'I have had no hospital training nor any nursing engagements
whatever.' References were supplied by Miss Gibson of Laurel
Court and Mrs Annette Roberts of Brinton Hall, East Dereham
in Norfolk, who had known Edith for fifteen years.

Mrs Roberts described Edith as

> energetic and ready to adapt herself to circumstance
> ... of high moral tone and a good deal of self-reliance
> ... Naturally ready and as far as I can judge willing to

follow guidance ... I have always formed a high opinion
of Edith Cavell and am glad of any opportunity of doing
her service, and giving her my recommendation.

She was to be criticized later by the Matron of the London
Hospital for this 'self-reliance'. One of matron Eva Lückes's
reports on Edith said: 'Edith Cavell was somewhat superficial,
and this characteristic naturally impressed itself upon her
work, which was by no means thorough. She had a self-
sufficient manner, which was very apt to prejudice people
against her.'

But with hundreds of patients to care for, the Fountain
Hospital was obviously keen to take on someone who was
teachable but able to work with minimal supervision.

There was no state register of nurses, and each teaching
hospital awarded their own certificates, so nursing standards
varied. Rates of pay were low. Until 1820, literacy wasn't a
requirement for nurses. The work was seen as lower than that
of a servant, and nurses had a reputation for being unhygienic,
dishonest, and addicted to alcohol. They worked for sixteen
hours in twenty-four. It was not seen as a respectable job for a
young woman.

But Victorian reforms were changing conditions for the
poorest in society. In 1867, a single Metropolitan Asylum
District was created in London for paupers 'who may be
infected with or suffering from fever, or the disease of smallpox
or may be insane'.

Smallpox epidemics in the 1880s led to further reforms, and
workhouse infirmaries were developed following the Diseases
Prevention Act of 1883 to treat paupers in the same hospitals

as those who could afford to pay for treatment, although there might be separate wards for those with sufficient money.

Unlike the Victorian workhouses, which were run by lay masters and their wives in a manner Charles Dickens described in vivid and sometimes gruesome detail, infirmaries such as the Fountain Hospital were staffed by a qualified medical superintendent with medically qualified assistants. They were required to admit any patient who was normally resident in the district. Standards of care were improving dramatically, but workhouse infirmaries still could not compete with the voluntary hospitals, which could turn away patients if the wards were full or if they did not find the patient's illness interesting and worthy of their superior care.

Workhouse conditions were not unfamiliar to Edith. Her father was chaplain to the Swainsthorpe workhouse near her home. But rapid advances in infection control made the infirmaries quite different from workhouses where paupers lived and worked. Stringent cleanliness and fresh air were the key components of patient care. However, sterilized medical gloves were not used for operations until the 1890s, and one in four patients admitted died in an infirmary.

Christian philanthropist Elizabeth Fry had made dramatic changes in the conditions of prisoners and people living in poverty in the first half of the nineteenth century. As well as her work in prisons, she established a night shelter for the destitute in London, and a district visiting society in Brighton to alleviate the plight of the poor. In 1840 she opened a training school for nurses, and her nurses were among those recruited by Florence Nightingale to care for wounded soldiers in the Crimean War.

Florence Nightingale's reforms dramatically reduced the death rate of wounded soldiers. Diseases such as typhus, cholera, and dysentery were the main reasons why the death rate was so high for soldiers in the Crimea. When the war ended in March 1856, 4,000 of the 94,000 men sent to the war area had died of their wounds, but 19,000 had died of diseases. The 'Lady with the Lamp', as Florence was known, devoted her life to improving the standard of nursing care, first in military hospitals and then in the infirmaries.

Edith was thrown into work at the Fountain Hospital with no training. Three months later she applied for a formal training place at the London Hospital. This time in addition to the reference from Mrs Roberts, she supplied a reference from Miss Dickenson, matron of the Fountain Hospital. Miss Dickenson confirmed that she was suitable for training as a hospital nurse, describing her as 'orderly, methodical and of kindly and gentle disposition'.

The voluntary hospitals such as 'the London' were funded by contributions from wealthy benefactors. They attracted the best doctors and the famous surgeons of the day; only top students were selected for training, and the hospitals were selective about which patients were admitted.

The London Hospital in the slum district of Whitechapel, founded in 1740, had had a chequered history in the decades before Edith arrived to start her training. It had famous surgeons including Frederick Treves who took care of Joseph Merrick, known as 'the Elephant Man' until he died at the London Hospital in 1890. Treves earned such a good living as a surgeon that he resigned from his position at the London in 1898, when he was only forty-five, in order to practise privately.

In 1902, he performed emergency surgery for appendicitis on King Edward VII, two days before the king was due to be crowned. But these glory days were still to come. In the 1870s the hospital was short of funds, short of nurses, and lacked the necessary nurses' accommodation to employ more.

The situation began to change when Miss Eva Lückes was appointed matron at the age of twenty-six in 1880. She played a significant part in the appointment of Sydney Holland to the London Hospital committee. Together they made an excellent team. As treasurer and chair, Holland raised the money for a substantial hospital expansion. Eva Lückes began a two-year training course for nurses who were accommodated in a new nurses' home, opened in 1895. She also started a nurses' library, and cookery classes to improve patients' diet, as well as a sickroom for her nurses so they need not be accommodated on the public ward if they fell ill. Hospital beds of a standard height and size were introduced to the wards in 1897 replacing old, mismatched bedsteads which were difficult to keep clean.

The new school for nurses was based in Tredegar House in Bow, East London, 'to soften the ordeal of the first beginning of hospital life for newcomers', according to Miss Lückes. Their training began with theory and demonstrations of practical procedures, with lectures on anatomy, bacteriology, hygiene, and physiology.

Edith started her training at the London Hospital's Preliminary Training School on 3 September 1896. The initial training, which was extended from six to seven weeks in the year Edith started, was in Miss Lückes's words, a

> pause on the threshold [which] gave eager beginners
> time and opportunity to realize the importance of the
> new life and work on which they are about to enter,
> work that is taken up far too lightly by many sadly
> lacking the necessary vocation.

Of the probationers who started training, some left and others were asked to leave if they were considered unsuitable. Edith was accepted for work on the wards and copied out two quotations to keep by her at Tredegar House: the verse from Longfellow's *A Psalm of Life* on leaving 'footprints on the sands of time' and lines from Milton's *Paradise Lost*:

> Not love thy life
> Nor hate, but whilst thou livest
> Live well

She began work in the main hospital at the end of 1896, just before her thirty-first birthday. The day began with a bell rung at 6 a.m. Breakfast was at 6.30 a.m. and duty on the ward started at 7 a.m. with prayers. Bible readings and prayers started and ended days on the wards as they had for Edith at home in Swardeston and at Laurel Court.

The prayers at the London Hospital were written on a card so patients could take part with the responsive readings. The nurses knelt around the ward to pray on small kneelers. Death and eternity were recurring themes in the prayers which Edith would have repeated morning and evening. They included a general confession, a prayer for pardon: 'so daily growing in grace and increasing in thy Holy Spirit more and more, we may at length come to thine everlasting kingdom, through Jesus Christ our Lord'.

Short prayers included the words: 'In sickness and in pain; in poverty and distress, in loneliness and weariness; in our dying hour, and in the great judgement day, Good Lord, deliver us...'; The Lord's Prayer, with the words, 'Thy kingdom come...' and a prayer for a 'blessing on remedies', 'that, after this painful life ended, we may inherit those unfading joys which thou hast prepared for them that love and obey thee'.

Prayers of thanksgiving included 'gratitude to the Benefactors and Patrons' and prayer for similar institutions 'that they may tend to unite all classes together in bonds of love and good-will and Christian charity'.

In the evenings there were two additional prayers for 'protection during the night' and 'for sleep'.

For Edith, these prayers were not simply a ritual. Prayer for patients was part of Edith's care for them. Colleagues noticed Edith standing and praying at patients' bedsides. Her patients were also active in their Christian faith. Mrs Alice Bancroft-Giggins told biographer Rowland Ryder about Edith's care for a relative, John Bancroft. He was operated on for paralysis of the spine without an anaesthetic, and Edith was his chief nurse. He brought his Bible with him to hospital and while Edith sat with him for thirty-six hours after his operation, she painted a spray of apple blossom on its flyleaf. She also added a quotation from *The Imitation of Christ*: 'If thou canst hold thy peace and suffer then shalt thou see without doubt the help of the Lord.'

Nurses at the London were allowed half an hour for lunch. There was tea on the ward, and supper when they went off duty at 9.20 p.m. They were allowed two hours off duty during the day, a day off once a fortnight, and two weeks holiday a year. This time off increased for more senior nurses. The probationers had to use some of their off-duty time to attend lectures.

A nurse's daily duties included keeping the wards swept and free of dust, a challenging task in itself as there were large open fires in the wards which needed tending and cleaning. The ward sister looked after two wards, fifty-six beds in all, and had her bedroom and sitting room on the ward, enabling her to keep constant watch on the nurses and their patients.

Emma Fraser, a contemporary of Edith, said, 'There was little or no social life with the minimum of opportunity for it, nurses were strictly forbidden to go out with doctors or medical students, and if discovered doing so the penalty was great.' Instant dismissal awaited anyone who contravened this strict rule.

Leisure activities included time in the hospital garden, known as the 'Garden of Eden', tended by the hospital gardener, nicknamed Adam, coincidently like Laurel Court. He was the only man allowed in the nurses' garden. Occasionally there were bus rides or boat trips on the Thames. Miss Lückes kept in touch with her staff with weekly 'At Homes' on Tuesday evenings from 7 p.m. to 9 p.m., when some of the 600 nurses were invited for tea and a bun in her sitting room.

Edith made some lasting friendships at the London. Fellow nurses Fanny Edgecombe and Bessie Leonard both joined the training school at about the same time as Edith, and the trio became known to other nurses as 'The Three Graces'. Fanny had worked in a hospital in Liverpool and Bessie, an Austrian by birth, had nursed at Queen Charlotte's Hospital. Both left nursing to get married in the early 1900s.

In the summer of 1897 a typhoid fever epidemic broke out in Maidstone, and Edith was one of the six nurses from the London Hospital who were sent to help. Around 250 nurses cared for the 1,700 patients who contracted the disease. Of these 132 died, but the outbreak was contained and the whole town was grateful.

Lilian Quinell was just five years old when she developed typhoid. Later she recalled Edith's nursing care: 'I always think of the lovely toys she brought me,' she told Rowland Ryder. 'I can still remember her driving away from our home at Dover Street in her pony and trap.'

After the epidemic was under control, Edith took Lilian and three other children to St Leonards-on-Sea in East Sussex to convalesce. She also dressed dolls in nurses' uniforms to display in the window of her lodgings, which she shared with another London Hospital nurse, Caroline Mary Ball. 'Carrie', as she was known, wrote a Christmas letter to her sister Elise on 10 December 1897 and mentioned Edith, describing her as 'a lady, mercifully, and we hit it off fairly well, considering we live in such close proximity'.

Their landlords owned a toyshop and the two nurses were lodged in a bedroom reached through a long show room which displayed the Christmas toys. Carrie's comment about Edith to her sister was: 'She reminds me of Father in the way she goes to bed – simply walks out of her clothes – leaving them where they are and walks into bed – she complains that I do paddle round such a time.'

Edith and Carrie seem to have worked night shifts throughout their eight weeks in Maidstone, as Carrie wrote: 'I think eight weeks without a night in bed rather stultifies my brains.'

When the epidemic was over, the appreciative people of Maidstone held a grand reception in the nurses' honour. The event was hosted by the mayor and mayoress of Maidstone and attended by the Lord Mayor of London and the mayors of six neighbouring towns. Each nurse was presented with a silver medal to show the town's 'gratitude for loving services' – the only medal Edith received in her lifetime.

After the presentation and speeches there was time for music, refreshments, and 'cinematographs' showing Queen Victoria's Diamond Jubilee celebrations, and pelicans being fed at London Zoo. However, Carrie and Edith had to leave to get back in time for night duty so missed the entertainment.

Once the work in Maidstone ended, Edith returned to the London Hospital and completed her two years' training. She gained her London Hospital certificate in September 1898, but Miss Lückes's report was not entirely encouraging. She wrote:

> Edith Cavell has plenty of capability when she choose
> to exert herself, but she is not much in earnest, not
> at all punctual ... and not a nurse that can altogether
> be depended upon. She did good work during the
> typhoid epidemic at Maidstone, and had sufficient
> ability to become a fairly good nurse by the end of
> her training. Her theoretical work was superior to her
> practical work. She attained only an average standard
> in the latter, giving the impression that she would have
> attained a higher one, if she had put her whole heart
> into it. I thought her best fitted for the private staff, and
> she was accordingly appointed in that capacity for her
> third year of service.

Later, writing a reference for Edith, Miss Lückes was less harsh in her assessment, describing Edith as 'thoroughly interested in her work'.

Miss Lückes set high standards and rarely gave a glowing report, but this did not limit Edith's admiration and respect for her mentor. She kept in touch with Miss Lückes as her career progressed. In 1903, when she wrote to Miss Lückes from the St Pancras Infirmary where she worked for about three years, she said: 'I have been very happy here on the whole and shall be sorry to leave ... but no place will ever be to me what the "London" was nor any matron like the one under whom I trained.'

In 1904 she wrote again to Miss Lückes, this time from the Shoreditch Infirmary: 'It will always be my most earnest endeavor to keep before the nurses under me the high standard under which I worked in my own days of training at the "London"'.

And in 1906 she wrote from Swardeston vicarage:

> I was staying with my brother-in-law, Dr Wainwright, at Henley recently and wished you could have heard the flattering things he and Dr Wallace, the Surgeon, said of your nurses – some from other places suffered much in comparison. I was asked to account for the difference and was very glad to have the opportunity of telling them of your lectures and personal influence and of the tone prevailing in our Hospital. They seem particularly struck by the ready way in which they (the nurses) accommodate themselves to circumstances and were willing to keep the patient's room in order and to give

as little trouble as possible. They spoke highly too of the
sick room cookery and of the nurses' ability to explain
to the cook how things should be made – I still keep my
own lectures on that and other subjects and have found
them useful over and over again.

During her year in private nursing, Edith moved from patient
to patient, nursing them in their homes as far afield as Iford
near Lewes in East Sussex, Marlborough in Wiltshire, Woburn
in Bedfordshire, and Newnham on Severn in Gloucestershire.

Her final post at the London Hospital was a year nursing in
Mellish Ward, a men's surgical ward, where she was appointed
staff nurse on 31 December 1899 to see in the start of the new
century. The sister in charge of Mellish Ward was four years
younger than Edith, and had started training a year after her.

Miss Lückes wrote in her records that Edith

was not a success as a Staff Nurse. She was convinced
that the Sister has a prejudice against her and after
carefully going into the matter I could not but fear
there were some ground for this conviction. At the
same time, E. S. Cavell [Edith sometimes used the
family name Scott] was not methodical nor observant
and she over-estimated her own powers. Her
intentions were excellent and she was conscientious
without being quite reliable as a nurse. If E. S. Cavell
had been happier in her ward I do not think she would
have wished to leave the hospital. She would have been
much better advised to resume Private Nursing but
this she did not wish to do. It appeared to me best on

the whole that she should have a change of work. E. S.
Cavell was steady and nice minded.

To resolve the situation, Miss Lückes recommended Edith for a post at the St Pancras Infirmary as night superintendent, where Miss Moir was matron.

Miss Lückes wrote:

> Miss Moir was specially anxious about this time that
> I should recommend her two Night Superintendents
> … I thought Nurse Berridge and E. S. Cavell would
> make an excellent combination and work well
> together and I recommended them accordingly.
> They obtained the appointments and E. S. Cavell left
> January 3, 1901.

Although it was not a happy year, Edith made a lasting friendship in this final phase at the London. Nurse Eveline Dickinson remained a firm friend for several years, and they occasionally spent holidays together until Eveline married and moved with her husband to Enniskillen in Ireland in 1906.

A month after Edith started in her new role, the Commonwealth was plunged into mourning at the death of Queen Victoria. Flags flew at half-mast. Official letters were written on black-edged paper and black armbands were worn. At the start of February 1901, Queen Victoria's coffin was taken from Osborne House on the Isle of Wight, where she had died, to Frogmore Mausoleum near Windsor Castle. Above the mausoleum's doors, Queen Victoria had inscribed in memory of her beloved Prince Albert, '*Vale desideratissime.* Farewell most beloved. Here at length I shall rest with thee, with thee in Christ I shall rise again.'

The Borough of St Pancras, Edith's new environment, was home to 235,317 people in 1901, and 6,307 were listed as paupers. Edith could have followed Miss Lückes's advice nursing private patients in relative comfort. Instead she chose a Poor Law hospital in a poverty-stricken area, and she worked night shifts. Less than ten weeks into the role, she started applying for other jobs.

In the summer, she was mugged on her way back to the hospital from a day in the country, and her purse was stolen. Shortly after this incident, she did have a month's break from night shifts, when she was appointed temporary matron of the Cheshunt Cottage Hospital while the permanent matron was on holiday.

Nightshifts alienate workers from normal life, but Edith did make friends with a colleague at St Pancras. Margaret Stone also enjoyed walking, and the pair would walk up to thirty miles in a day. Rickmansworth was a favourite destination.

Eventually, in November 1903 she found a new job as assistant matron at the Shoreditch Infirmary. She wrote to Miss Lückes: 'I am glad to have obtained some day work after my three years on night duty.' Evidently she had a career path in mind, as she added:

> I hope the position will provide a help for the future, and the salary is better than the one I am receiving at the present. I am glad to know that I shall have much supervision of the wards under Miss Inglis and shall be able to teach the probationers and improve their work.

> I shall also have charge of the linen room and have to
> overlook the laundry. It will be a new experience and I
> hope to learn much from it.

The hospital had begun as the infirmary for the St Leonard Shoreditch workhouse, which opened in 1777. Dr James Parkinson, who gave his name to Parkinson's disease, worked at the hospital from 1813 and established a separate fever block within the infirmary for patients with infectious diseases, such as cholera. In the 1860s the hospital was rebuilt with wards that were separate from the main workhouse. But the workhouse remained open until 1930.

The matron, Miss Joan Inglis, said of Edith:

> I liked her, I admired her unswerving sense of duty,
> but I never felt close to her. Kindliness and a charming
> personality made her loved by her nurses and patients,
> but I never knew anyone who felt that she really
> understood Edith Cavell. One felt, somehow, that she
> had hidden resources within her. Her reserved manner
> in another person would have appeared to be snobbery,
> but in Edith Cavell it was a grave dignity that filled her
> associates with deep admiration for her.

Edith used her off-duty time to visit patients at home. This was an innovation on Edith's part as, at the time, nursing did not involve home visits or follow-up work once a patient had been discharged from hospital.

Although Edith enjoyed the opportunity to teach, she was still on the lookout for more responsible work. In

November 1904, she applied for the matron's role at Ventnor's Consumption Hospital, but without success.

By 1906, she had been nursing for ten years with only the briefest of holiday breaks. Her London Hospital friend Eveline Dickinson was engaged to be married that September, and wanted to go on holiday with Edith, possibly travelling in Europe for a few months from April or May. Edith needed a break, but was worried that she would not be able to find another suitable post on her return. She wrote again to Miss Lückes: 'Would you very kindly help me in August – when I should be ready to return to work – if I wrote to you then?'

When she resigned from her role at Shoreditch Hospital, the nurses gave her a sapphire pendant set with pearls as a leaving gift. She was so embarrassed to be given so much attention that she chose to receive the gift from the matron, Miss Inglis, in her office rather than at the nurses' home. Finally, she had a holiday. She spent some time in Cornwall with Eveline, before they set off on their travels to Italy, France, and Switzerland. They ended their summer in London, where Edith helped Eveline to buy her trousseau before she got married.

By 13 September 1906, Edith was back in Swardeston for her sister Lilian's thirty-sixth birthday. True to her word, she wrote again to Miss Lückes: 'I have been trying for some time to obtain a post of trust as Matron or Superintendent in an Institution, but so far without success…'

That month she was given a temporary post as a Queen's district nurse at the Manchester and Salford Sick Poor and Private Nursing Institution. The role was originally for just six weeks, but the matron became ill and Edith was asked to take charge. She explained her new situation in her next letter to Eva Lückes, on 12 March 1907. The matron would be out of action for several months: 'I feel it rather a heavy responsibility...' Edith wrote.

The Manchester job was a turning point for Edith. A job offer came out of the blue in May, and in June she updated Miss Lückes: 'I am writing to tell you that I have just accepted a permanent appointment in Brussels...' Her teaching ability, nursing abilities, and proficiency in French had combined to open up a new chapter in her life.

CHAPTER 7

IMAGES OF HEAVEN

LISTEN, I TELL YOU A MYSTERY: WE WILL NOT ALL SLEEP, BUT WE
WILL ALL BE CHANGED – IN A FLASH, IN THE TWINKLING OF AN
EYE, AT THE LAST TRUMPET. FOR THE TRUMPET WILL SOUND, THE
DEAD WILL BE RAISED IMPERISHABLE …

(1 Corinthians 15:51–52)

Nursing in London's East End highlighted Edith's awareness of
mortality, so that on the last night before her execution she was
able to say: 'I have seen death so often that it is not strange or
fearful to me.'

To understand Edith's confidence in the face of death, we
need to appreciate the Victorian and Edwardian mindset, and
the influences which gave them a strong and sustaining image
of heaven.

Several factors contributed to the Victorian awareness
and acceptance of death. Queen Victoria spent four decades
of mourning after Prince Albert died in 1861. She refused to
appear in public for three years after his death, and wore black
until she died in 1901.

Perhaps as a result, mourning was elevated to an art form.
Victorian funeral rituals were elaborate and costly, with the

richest families transporting the coffin to the grave in a glass carriage drawn by black, plumed horses. Affluent families erected ostentatious monuments to their loved ones. They used black-edged stationery throughout the period of mourning, and they could even buy mourning teapots, black crêpe to cover the brass knocker on their door, and mourning umbrellas. Mourners wore special black mourning clothes and widows wore black for two years, avoiding social contact, and refusing invitations.

Friendly societies and burial clubs developed so poorer people could save for a 'decent burial'. The alternative for paupers was burial in a mass grave, or their body could be used for dissection in an anatomy school.

Tuberculosis accounted for around a third of all deaths from disease in the Victorian era. Overcrowding and the lack of hygiene meant it was difficult to prevent it spreading, and there was no effective treatment. Infant mortality was high, with the average family having five children, with only two or three surviving to adulthood. In the 1900s, a third of deaths occurred in the under-fives (compared with less than 1 per cent in Britain today). As mentioned earlier, life expectancy was forty-seven for men and fifty for women, so Edith's death at forty-nine was not unusually early – though the manner of her death shocked the nation.

The Victorian acceptance of death was matched by an assurance of an eternal destiny. When Dickens described the death of Little Nell in *The Old Curiosity Shop*, he expressed the Victorian confidence that heaven is a far better place than life on earth. He writes:

> Think what earth is, compared with the World to which
> her young spirit has winged its early flight; and say, if one
> deliberate wish expressed in solemn terms above this
> bed could call her back to life, which of us would utter it!

Every day of Edith's life had been infused with the belief that death is not the end. Morning and evening prayers declared that Jesus has risen from death and has ascended to heaven, and that resurrection and everlasting life awaits Jesus' followers.

The Bible reading at Queen Victoria's funeral from 1 Corinthians 15:20–58 summed up that certainty with familiar words which are echoed in other well-known literary and musical works such as John Donne's 'Holy Sonnets' and Handel's *Messiah*.

> Listen, I tell you a mystery: we will not all sleep, but
> we will all be changed – in a flash, in the twinkling of
> an eye, at the last trumpet. For the trumpet will sound,
> the dead will be raised imperishable, and we will be
> changed. For the perishable must clothe itself with the
> imperishable, and the mortal with immortality. When
> the perishable has been clothed with the imperishable,
> and the mortal with immortality, then the saying that is
> written will come true: 'Death has been swallowed up
> in victory.'
>
> 'Where, O death, is your victory?
> Where, O death, is your sting?'
>
> The sting of death is sin, and the power of sin is the law.
> But thanks be to God! He gives us the victory through
> our Lord Jesus Christ. (1 Corinthians 15:51–57)

Edith's vision of heaven was informed by these and other Bible verses from her daily readings, as well as the books she read, such as *The Pilgrim's Progress*. In the new century, a second royal funeral in 1910 and the two coronations of 1902 and 1911 also portrayed a vision of heaven.

British coronations are full of rich symbolism drawn from the Bible. The monarch arrives at Westminster Abbey in scarlet robes to emulate Christ's sacrifice. A simple linen robe is worn for the anointing. This shows that the monarchy is not an inherited or earned right, but a gift from God, empowered by his Holy Spirit. For the final procession, the monarch leaves the abbey wearing a purple cloak to indicate royalty. Trumpets, anthems, and cheering crowds are all part of the ceremony, shadows of what the apostle John said we can expect in heaven. Thousands gather to pay homage, reminiscent of Daniel's vision of the thousands attending the 'Ancient of Days' (Daniel 7:9–14).

Today these Bible passages have been forgotten by the majority of the population, but most Victorians attended church most Sundays. Those who, like Edith, used the Book of Common Prayer on a daily basis, read the passage in Daniel every year on 18 September as part of the calendar of Bible readings. The book of Revelation was read every December. Seeing the pageantry of royal occasions enacted reinforced what they read in the Bible about what was to come after death.

The description of heaven in John's Revelation includes people from every race standing before God's throne. Edward VII's June 1902 coronation was postponed as he was taken ill and needed emergency surgery, so many of the royal visitors and dignitaries from around the world had returned home before Edward was crowned on 9 August. But his funeral in May 1910, a few weeks before Edith's own father died, was attended by eight visiting European monarchs: King Haakon VII of Norway, Tsar Ferdinand of the Bulgarians, King Manuel II of Portugal and the Algarve, Kaiser Wilhelm II of Germany and Prussia, King George I of the Hellenes, King Albert I of the Belgians, King Alfonso XIII of Spain, and King Frederick VIII of Denmark, as well as the new King George V of the United Kingdom.

George V's coronation in 1911 was also an international affair with visitors gathered from many nations, races, and languages, again giving people a foretaste of a heavenly reality. Even if Edith was not among the thousands who lined the route for these national events, she is likely to have seen a cinema newsreel of Edward VII and George V's coronations. By 1910, *Pathé's Animated Gazette* was showing weekly newsreels to 10 million viewers. Also, newspapers included lengthy eyewitness reports.

The Bishop of Durham attended both coronations. He described Edward VII's coronation as

> a sight, of such a scene, so vast, well ordered, splendid,
> so full of a mighty history, and the possibility of
> a wonderful future in the mercy of God: and so
> richly filled, alike by its solemn delay and its glad
> accomplishment with the sense of the power and grace
> of the King Eternal.

He also described George V's coronation, in particular the sermon:

> The glory of service was its theme; the service of God,
> in serving man; the call to the highest, in the footsteps
> of the Most High who humbled Himself, to see in the
> Crown the symbol of supreme self-sacrifice.

At the start of the twentieth century, the Christian faith was still part of the fabric of British life. Just as the king was called to serve as a follower of Christ, Edith's nursing career was also a call to serve others as a follower of Jesus who humbled himself.

The Bishop of Durham also described the presentation of a Bible to the king as a key part of the coronation service.

> The Holy Bible, lying massive on its cushion, was held
> before the King for his acceptance, with these few
> weighty words; 'Our Gracious King, we present you
> with this Book, the most valuable thing that this world
> affords. Here is wisdom; this is the Royal Law; these are
> the lively oracles of God.'

Although the coronation regalia include some of the most valuable gems in the world, this part of the ceremony, which was also part of Queen Elizabeth's coronation, emphasizes that the Bible is more valuable than all the world's gems. For Edith and millions of others living through this Edwardian era, the Bible was part of everyday life, providing a code to live by.

Quite apart from the pageantry of royal occasions, Edith was surrounded by images of heaven, which confirmed what she read in the Bible. The Victorian enthusiasm for plant-collecting meant the gardens being planted in stately homes and Victorian villas included exotic species from around the world, such as those seen by Edith in her visit to Frankfurt's Palmengarten.

The beautiful garden is a perpetual image of heaven with its echoes of Eden, the symbolism of a 'promised land flowing with milk and honey' and foretaste of heaven with its 'tree of life, bearing twelve crops of fruit, yielding its fruit every month' (Revelation 22:2).

The crowded, smoke-filled slums of London contrasted with the image of heaven, 'the Holy City', with its walls of jasper, foundations decorated with precious stones, gates of pearls, and streets of gold as described in John's Revelation. Also the garden city movement, which began at the end of the nineteenth century, aimed to create a utopian combination of town and country instead of crowded and unhealthy cities.

Even war reinforced the imagery of heaven, as Christians looked forward to the last battle and the beginning of Christ's eternal reign of peace. As the Gospel of Matthew underlined:

> You will hear of wars and rumours of wars …
> Nation will rise against nation, and kingdom against
> kingdom. There will be famines and earthquakes in
> various places. … And this gospel of the kingdom
> will be preached in the whole world as a testimony
> to all nations, and then the end will come. (Matthew
> 24:6–7, 14)

And the final victory:

> Then will appear the sign of the Son of Man in heaven
> … the Son of Man coming on the clouds of heaven,

> with power and great glory. And he will send his angels
> with a loud trumpet call ... (Matthew 24:30–31).

Edith may well have watched the Boer War Victory Parade that took place in London in 1902, wondering if wars and rumours of wars were the beginning of the end.

CHAPTER 8

NEW BEGINNINGS IN BELGIUM

NURSING MUST ALWAYS BE SOMETHING MORE THAN A
MERE PROFESSION, IT MUST BE LOVE INSPIRED AS WELL AS
TECHNICALLY EFFICIENT.

(Eva Lückes, matron of the London Hospital and Edith's mentor)

In 1907, while the nursing profession was developing rapidly
in Britain, just across the English Channel in Belgium, little had
changed in nursing since medieval times. Hospitals were run
by the church, with nuns looking after the patients. Spiritual
care was given priority over physical care. Cleanliness was not
considered important, and the nuns had no training to nurse
the sick or injured. Private nurses could be hired by the rich, but
were untrained and considered lower than the lowest servant,
just as they had been in England a century earlier.

But one leading Belgian surgeon, Dr Antoine Depage, had
begun to take action. He had risen from humble beginnings
and gained a university scholarship, later becoming a university
professor and eminent surgeon in Brussels. On one occasion,
when he did succeed in training a nun to assist him in the
operating theatre, her mother superior suddenly ordered her
away from the hospital to be replaced with another nun with no

hospital experience. Dr Depage was exasperated. He resorted to recruiting nurses from Sweden, Germany, Denmark, and Holland to help him with surgery, as there were no nurses being trained in Belgium.

Short on tact or patience, Depage's solution was to start an independent nursing school, free from political or church ties. To do this, he brought together doctors, businessmen, and lawyers to start a nursing school council, and a ladies' committee formed of well-connected and affluent women. Together they agreed to set up a school to provide doctors with trained nurses and to open up a new career for young, educated women.

Fundraising began, and adjacent houses in a suburb in the south of Brussels were identified as a suitable base. Having established the vision and found the premises, the next task was to find a matron. Dr Depage wanted the school to be run in the style of Florence Nightingale's school in England, but they needed a matron who was fluent in French and with an ability to understand the Belgian temperament.

One of the ladies' committee members, Madam Graux, was the mother-in-law of Marguerite, one of the François children to whom Edith had been a governess. Marguerite had married Madam Graux's son, Pierre. The François family had kept in touch with their governess and were aware of her successful career as a nurse. As a result, Edith was contacted and invited to become matron of Belgium's first nurses' training school.

In June 1907, Edith wrote to her mentor, Eva Lückes:

> I am writing to tell you that I have just accepted a
> permanent appointment in Brussels. I had a letter some
> time ago asking me if I would consent to become the

Matron of the first training school of nurses out there, which is to be opened in October. Up to the present they have only had nuns to nurse the sick, and they are often ignorant and the lay nurses always dirty. They have formed two committees – one of ladies and the other of well-known doctors and lawyers – so that I think it should be a success, particularly as some of the best-known names there are connected with them. [Edith's five years in Brussels working for one of the city's affluent families meant she knew the 'best-known' families.] They are anxious that the school should be carried on on English lines, and that the head of it should be an Englishwoman knowing their language and manner of life. We shall begin with a few pupils (I have made a point of educated women as the first trained nurses will become the teachers ultimately) and a few patients, and it will, I hope, develop rapidly into a fair-sized training school. Looking forward I hope that in time both private and district nursing may spring from this beginning as the need for both is, I believe greatly felt, and people are no longer willing to put up with the old class of nurse. I am going over to Brussels in August to get everything in readiness, and hope that I shall be allowed to engage a trained night-superintendent ...

The post was perfect for Edith. She had lived in Brussels, and spoke fluent French. She had worked in a variety of different hospitals, and had gained a wide range of experience, the most recent as a matron in Manchester. Her nursing skill, combined with her teaching ability, hard work and organizing zeal were the ideal gifts to bring to this new and demanding role.

The next few months didn't quite meet up to Edith's high expectations, however. Her start date was delayed, and on 19 September she wrote again to Miss Lückes:

> I arrived two days ago and found the four houses, which have been made to communicate, only partly furnished and in much confusion. The Council were all absent on holiday, except the Secretary and the President who returned for a day or two to welcome me. No servants – only a portress – and nothing furnished but my sitting room! And we have to open on October the 1st!

Anyone else might have postponed the opening. Not Edith. She could see the need and the challenges: 'Everyone is very keen but very indefinite', she wrote to Miss Lückes. 'They make notes of things needed but there it ends. I hope to pull through, however, and to have a model school.'

The four adjacent houses in the rue de la Culture, which formed the *École Belge d'infirmières Diplômées* – the Belgian nurses' training school – were in the quiet Brussels suburb of Ixelles. The area would have been familiar to Edith, as the François family home was in Avenue Louise, which divides the area in two. When completed, the houses included Edith's private rooms, including her bedroom, a sitting room and an office, the nurses' bedrooms, their sitting room, and dining room. The kitchen, linen rooms, and laundry were in the basement. Unfortunately this was damp and crawling with cockroaches and there were no lifts, so meals had to be carried on trays up steep stairs. There was an out-patients' surgery, wards with five beds in each, private patients' rooms, a waiting room, and a lecture room. Bathrooms were also used as sterilizing rooms with saucepans on gas rings to boil the water to sterilize the instruments. The operating theatre was inconveniently situated on the top floor to ensure the best possible light, but patients had to be carried on stretchers up and down stairs.

These adapted private houses were not an ideal setting, but Edith set the same high standards of cleanliness and order as were to be found at the London Hospital. Even after war broke out and they had few patients, she insisted that every ward should be dusted daily.

Edith was involved in every aspect of the school's life, designing the school's emblem – a white edelweiss on a green background – and the nurses' uniforms. These were light blue with high white linen aprons, and starched white collars, sleeves, and 'Sister Dora' caps. These caps were named after Dorothy Wyndlow Pattison. Also a daughter of a vicar, Sister Dora joined the Sisterhood of the Good Samaritans in Middlesbrough in 1864, and devoted her life to nursing the people of Walsall in the West Midlands. When she died in 1878, the town erected a statue in her honour.

The 'Sister Dora' cap was made to a very precise design cut from one piece of cloth with a three-inch hem to turn over in front, and narrow tape around the back so it could be gathered and tied to fit the back of the head. Stiff, white, stand-up, linen collars were required wearing, not the soft, turned-down, white linen collar favoured by some nurses. White linen oversleeves, fastened at the cuff with a button and with elastic at the elbow, covered the nurses' bare forearms and could be washed separately to maintain high standards of cleanliness and infection control.

Edith wore a dark blue uniform, also with a starched white collar and cuffs and a severe white cap – though without the strings under the chin which are shown on her statue near London's Trafalgar Square, where she is depicted wearing the outdoor uniform of the London Hospital. Shoes were her one extravagance and colleagues remember they often had beautiful buckles.

Two weeks after the training school opened she wrote to Miss Lückes:

> Two of my pupils seem likely to make excellent nurses ... I find them unpunctual and rather noisy, but the patients are devoted to them, and we already have a reputation for nursing well! We have four patients at present and others coming.

She tried to instil the rigorous discipline which she had endured as a trainee, modelling herself on Miss Lückes, and the school on the London Hospital where she had been trained. Although she seemed starchy and formal at times, she was not as stern as Eva Lückes, and her trainee nurses were not as compliant as Edith's fellow trainees had been. Her nurses remember that each day one of them would be sent upstairs to put her cap on properly or called into Miss Cavell's office to put on their caps at the right angle in front of her. But kindness is one of the most common characteristics associated with her memory.

The first five nurses were recruited as probationers. Clara Böhme was twenty-three and had also been a governess in the Avenue Louise, to the Solvay family. (Madame Solvay was one of the ladies' committee.) Clara completed her training and remained in contact with the nurses' training hospital until she married. Noémie Delaunoy also completed her training. Hélène Stoops left the course after three years, but Emile Van de Velde and Valentine de Wolf only stayed a year. Emile was thirty-seven and decided that she was too old to work as a probationer; Valentine found the discipline too demanding.

The probationers signed on for five years' training. Pay was low by British nursing standards and hours were long: twelve hours on duty with only a half-day off duty each week and a full day off each month. A complete month's leave was granted once a year. Even the word 'duty' seemed a foreign concept to some of the nurses who had not grown up in England, where duty to God and to the reigning monarch were paramount. For Edith, her sense of duty gave her a heightened sense of responsibility for all those in her care, and for the development of Belgium's embryonic nursing profession. When a professional journal for Belgium's nurses was launched in 1910, Edith's first article was entitled, 'Duties of the Nurse'.

Biographer Helen Judson quotes one of her English nurses, who said:

> We staff nurses never ceased to marvel at the patience and understanding that she had for the Belgian probationers to whom nursing was so new. If she was discouraged with them, she never showed it; and she always told us that we must have more patience for

she said, 'In time they will catch the spirit and gain
the skill which they now lack.' However, from her
staff nurses, especially those who had been trained in
England she expected the best – no excuse saved you
if you were careless or slovenly, or fell short of your
professional duty.

It was not easy to recruit French-speaking, English-trained
nurses to work at the training hospital on low wages for long
hours, and on one occasion Dr Depage bypassed Edith and
hired three Dutch nurses 'as they do not expect so much salary'.

At the end of the first month of the school's life, Edith
wrote again to Miss Lückes, thanking her for recommending
Linda Maude as an assistant. Unfortunately, Linda's French
was not good enough to become a matron, so she was made
superintendent to the nurses.

Edith's regular letters to Eva Lückes often included a plea
for nurses. 'If you have anyone suitable that you could spare I
should be very glad.' On one occasion she wrote: 'I am afraid
I shall never be satisfied with any other than a "Londoner" to
train the probationers. Other methods do not please me and I
am anxious to introduce the very best to Belgium.'

Night shifts were a challenge for the new recruits. When
the five probationers came to sign their five-year contracts after
a three-month trial period, four of them refused to sign on
the basis that a month on night duty was too long. They said
it should be reduced to a week at a time. The training school
committee sided with the nurses against Edith's wishes, and
she had to allow the shift pattern to change to a week on night
shift at a time.

Edith wrote to Miss Lückes on 2 December 1907: 'I had thought to be lenient in proposing so short a period', she said. Several months on night duty, rather than weeks, was the norm at the London Hospital.

> However, I had eventually to yield, or see them all
> depart, in which case it would have become known that
> they left on account of the severity of the regulations.
> Then I should never have been able to get anyone else!

On 7 January 1908 she wrote again. 'The probationers are making more progress. I think they are beginning to regret their short night duty, but I am not appearing to know that at present...' Edith knew from experience that it takes time to adjust to night shifts, and a longer stint makes it easier to adapt to sleeping during the day and working at night.

The nurses soon learned to respect and admire their matron. Clara's vivid description of her first meeting with Edith is recorded by biographer Helen Judson.

> About three o'clock in the afternoon of a warm sunny
> day, in September, 1907, I arrived at No. 179, rue de
> la Culture, and was at once admitted to Miss Cavell's
> study.
>
> This study was the middle of three rooms, the front
> one giving a view onto the street, the third one leading
> out into a quiet garden, where birds were singing in the
> bushes. All the communicating doors were wide open,
> so that the study was quite full of the reflected sunshine
> from the garden.

Edith Cavell was seated at her desk, her small, capable, expressive hands folded before her. She wore a dress of soft dark blue material, relieved at the neck by a white starched collar. Her fine, dark brown hair, slightly grey at the temples, was neatly parted and arranged. Her beautiful, clear, grey eyes were kindly but direct and searching in their gaze. Her voice was low, agreeable, and cultured, and I found her command of French remarkably fluent.

I was at once attracted to her, and it was during that first interview that I was to receive the impression, which never left me, that everything around Edith Cavell, touching her near and far, the atmosphere of those rooms, the neatness of her attire, her attitudes, her poise, the words she used, all enhanced and conveyed what were perhaps her greatest characteristics: efficiency, thoroughness, serenity, and above all great kindliness.

Clara also told biographer Rowland Ryder: 'We were more like a family than anything else.' She refuted other people's descriptions of Edith as 'humourless'. 'You can't work with someone for five years without knowing whether she has a sense of humour,' Clara added. 'You can tell in all sorts of ways: Miss Cavell was gay.' (In the first half of the twentieth century, the word 'gay' meant 'carefree' and 'happy'.)

On one occasion, Valentine de Wolf left a bath tap running until the water overflowed and cascaded down the stairs. The nurses rushed to her aid to mop up the mess before Edith set off on her nightly round of the wards. Clara recalled, 'She turned back but with that inevitable twinkle in her eyes. I am sure she had at once taken in the situation and liked us all the more for our *esprit de corps*.'

Two days later, when they all went with Edith to the linen room, immediately below the bathroom, to get the clean linen for the week, the room smelt badly of damp and the ceiling plaster had turned grey. Clara said Miss Cavell looked up at the damp ceiling then at the nurses, but didn't say a word.

Evenings were often spent in matron's sitting room discussing the day's problems, but also singing together around the piano in the nurses' sitting room. Edith often joined the nurses on these occasions. For their first Christmas together, the ladies' committee provided a Christmas tree, and committee members visited the training hospital with gifts for the nurses. They gave Edith a kettle and stand, which was a minor triumph as, only three months earlier, the committee had tried to exert their authority over Edith and had objected to her offering her visitors tea when they came to call on her – an English tradition that didn't go down well with some of the ladies.

Nothing escaped Edith's eagle eye as she walked through the training hospital. But she taught by example, never expecting the nurses to do something she would not do herself, and always working longer and harder than any of them. As the school became established, her routine developed. Her day started with breakfast at 7 a.m. with the staff. This was followed by a meeting for the staff nurses in her sitting room to give out their orders for the day. Between 9 a.m. and 10 a.m. she was available for visitors from outside the school. She was present to assist the doctors at all operations, at whatever time they took place. Lunch was at 12.30 p.m. and she gave her lectures to student nurses for an hour after lunch or joined them for lectures given by the doctors.

The Belgian nurses were served with coffee at 4 p.m. and English nurses were served tea. Dinner was at 7 p.m., then Edith went through the nurses' written notes with them one by one in her office at the end of the day, making suggestions and corrections to maintain the highest standards of patient care.

Although no biographer mentions daily prayers in the wards, these are likely to have been part of every day, just as they had been at the London Hospital, where daily prayers continued on wards into the second half of the twentieth century.

Edith's training extended to the doctors and to the employees of private patients. Doctors had to be reminded to greet the nurses on the wards and to show respect to this new profession. It was more difficult to change the ingrained attitudes of people outside the training hospital. Once the nurses' training was completed some were employed as private nurses in family homes. The status of a nurse had been considered lower than any of the other household servants, so family servants sometimes refused to serve the nurses their meals. Edith had to change these ingrained attitudes by insisting that her private nurses had their meals served with members of the family.

In April 1908, Edith wrote an account of the school's first six months for the *Nursing Mirror*. She described the houses and the daily routine for the five nurses who each cared for five patients.

> One house had been fitted up as a home for twelve
> nurses. They have a sitting-room with a piano. Three

adjoining houses provide twenty-four bedrooms for patients each of whom pay 5-8 f. a day. There are gas rings in the bathrooms for boiling water and sterilizing instruments. Five pupils have had the courage to come forward, and they are already settling down to their new life and seem happy at their work. Each one has five patients to look after. They breakfast at 7 a.m. Then they wash their patients and give them their breakfasts. During the morning they accompany the doctor on his rounds and carry out the treatments which he orders. Our probationers must be between twenty and thirty-five years of age. They can be any nationality but French is spoken. Uniform is provided – out-door uniform is not worn – and they are paid 180 f. their first year, 240 f. their second, and 300 f. their third ...

She also outlined the training.

The first three years will be devoted entirely to training; the first in the school, mainly medical nursing; the second in a surgical clinic; the third to the nursing of infectious diseases and to midwifery. They will then be required to pass an examination and, if successful, will be granted diplomas after which they will be employed in private nursing homes, as the commitments of the school dictate.

Clear goals guided the training programme, which Edith described with pride.

The object of the school is threefold …

First, to create a profession for women; secondly, to forward the cause of science; thirdly, to provide the best possible help for the sick and suffering. These first nurses of ours will in the years which lie ahead teach, as no others have ever had the opportunity of doing, the laws of health and the methods of treating disease. They will also prove to their countrymen that education and position do not constitute a bar to an independent life for a woman, as so many seem to suppose over here. Indeed, they will show them that education and position are in point of fact good and solid foundations on which to build a career which demands the best and highest qualities that womanhood can offer.

By the end of 1908, the *École Belge d'infirmières Diplômées* had cared for fifty-seven patients, and plans were being made to expand the work further to other hospitals. The following year, twenty-three probationers started the training course, and the city authorities asked Edith to provide nurses to look after the children in all the city's state schools. In May 1909, another Londoner, Evelyn Hope-Bell, who was nursing a private patient in Brussels, wrote about Edith to a friend: 'Her work is so much liked by the top doctors and surgeons here…'

Dr Armand Colard, one of the doctors who saw how Edith worked, wrote in his 1954 account of the hospital, 'Success was now assured. Provincial hospitals, private clinics, suburban schools and general practitioners asked for our nurses.'

The vision was becoming a reality, and Edith's work in Belgium was gaining wide acclaim. In July 1909, she was invited to give a report on 'Nursing in Belgium' to the International Council of Nurses meeting in Church House, Westminster, London. As well as outlining the training programme, she said, 'A great point is made of discipline and character, and the pupils have given proof of much devotion and loyalty.'

There were thirteen probationers by this time, and trained nurses were also taken on to meet the growing demand. An extra house was added to the four to accommodate the extra staff. In their report on the work, the nursing school council wrote:

> Among the things that a nurse must learn is that
> there is much that cannot be taught by a professor.
> Even constant practice at the bedside is not enough.
> Character has to be shaped. A sense of responsibility
> has to be inculcated. This is achieved by the intimate
> evening talks which our Directress has with all
> her pupils. It is quality rather than quantity in the
> production of nurses at which we shall always aim.

Having the right attitude was key to the skills that nurses 'caught' from Edith Cavell. When it was decided that trained nurses were to be introduced to one of the church-run hospitals, Edith knew that the nuns would not find this easy. 'The conditions are not ideal', she wrote to Eva Lückes. 'Conflicts with the nuns would certainly take place if any one became Matron who had not sufficient tact.'

With the work expanding every year, there was little time for Edith to have a social life or to make friends apart from her colleagues. Her role as directress meant she had to remain detached, but she did attend church, the ecumenical Chapelle de la Résurrection, as she had previously, and she made friends with other English people in Brussels. Among these were Ernest and Norah Symons and their three children.

Their daughter Eileen remembered developing scarlet fever when she was nine in 1911. She told Rowland Ryder, 'I remember vividly being carried up the road wrapped in blankets, by my father in the dark of night with Miss Cavell's quick step beside us, and I was duly packed into bed.' A few days later, 'Miss Cavell made me a miniature uniform, a replica of the one worn by her nurses, and I was terribly proud of this.' Edith's good humour showed again in their story. Once when Eileen was wearing the uniform, Edith conspired with a doctor to treat the little girl as a nurse. He walked into the ward and said to Eileen, 'Good morning, nurse, where is my patient?' Eileen never forgot it.

Edith was particularly fond of children and animals. Dr Depage's sons remember playing in the gardens behind the training hospital. Pierre Depage told biographer Helen Judson,

> I remember we always counted it a privilege to be allowed to play in Miss Cavell's garden. We liked her and were not at all afraid of the serious, quiet, small lady whose eyes were so kind ... we wanted her to like us. I think she did, for we were always welcome in rue de la Culture.

Although she had no children of her own, Edith took in two young women who became like daughters to her. Edith's brother-in-law, Dr Longworth Wainwright, contacted her about one of his patients, a girl in her early twenties who had become addicted to morphine and needed a complete break. Edith agreed to take Grace Jemmett under her wing. This was not an easy task, as Grace was a chain smoker, and her craving for morphine made her devious and difficult at times. She also suffered severe bouts of depression, which kept her in bed for weeks at a time. But Edith gave her a home and cared for her, even though she faced criticism for her love and generosity when Grace was behaving badly. Grace responded to Edith's care and even called her 'Mother'.

In 1911 the chaplain at the Chapelle de la Résurrection, where Edith worshipped, contacted her about a young English girl called Pauline Randall, who had run away from her father who worked with a travelling circus. Edith agreed to give her a home. She was baptized and Edith became the thirteen-year-old's godmother. She arranged for her education, gave her work as a maid, paid money into a bank account for her, and also took her home to England when she went on holiday to Norfolk.

This unusual family was completed by Edith's pet dogs, Don and Jack. They were among the strays which Edith befriended and fed. Although the hospital committee was not pleased, Edith gave them a home. One of the nurses, Elisabeth Wilkins OBE, told biographer A. E. Clark-Kennedy, 'She loved flowers and animals, and was especially devoted to her Belgian sheepdog Jackie. He adored his mistress, but disliked strangers, and usually took a nip at any stranger if he got a chance.'

Speaking for the nurses, Jacqueline van Til said, 'We detested Jackie, who became even fiercer than Don, and would try to bite anyone who ever dared look at his mistress.'

Every life was sacred to Edith. When a probationer proposed to kill a large spider, Edith's response was don't kill it, take it outside: 'A nurse does not take life, she gives it.'

The sanctity of life, the duties of a nurse, and communication skills were among the wide range of subjects she covered with her student nurses, alongside practical nursing proficiency.

Throughout her years in Brussels, Edith made a point of returning home to visit her parents. Her father retired from ministry in Swardeston in 1909, and the elderly couple moved to a house in Norwich where Revd Cavell died a year later, only weeks after King Edward VII's death. Edith returned to Norfolk for her father's funeral at Swardeston parish church. Later that year, she was back in England to take her mother away on holiday to West Runton, on the north Norfolk coast. Mrs Cavell did visit Edith in Brussels, exploring the option of moving to live with her daughter there. But life outside England didn't suit her, so she returned to Norwich.

Edith continued to show concern for her mother's welfare. She wrote affectionate letters regularly, sent money several times a year and spent part of every annual holiday with her mother, often taking either Grace Jemmett or Pauline Randall with her.

But her work in Belgium was achieving her life's ambition, leaving her own 'footprints on the sands of time'. Edith had opened new hospitals at St Gilles, Jumet, and Foret with St Gilles staffed by her own trained nurses. Her goal was to make St Gilles '... a model in point of view of good order, cleanliness, and good nursing for the other hospitals in Belgium.'

When Dr Depage addressed the International Congress of Nurses in Cologne in 1912, he declared: 'Our School is the benchmark for nursing standards in Belgium.' And Edith's letter to Eva Lückes the following April, showed the impact of her efforts:

> ... the 'trained nurse' is making progress. All the new nursing homes and hospitals are engaging lay nurses now, and we have more demands than we can supply ... We have all the board schools under our supervision, with 12 nurses at work in them, and also a staff of 20 private nurses ...

Obviously proud of her achievements, she saved her best news until last in her letter to her mentor: 'My committee ... have raised the necessary funds to build us a new school ... we hope to be installed in about 2 years.'

Edith had set her sights high, to turn nursing into a profession in Belgium with the highest standards for trainees and a model hospital. An architect was commissioned to design the new training school and work began.

When Edith headed back to Norfolk for a well-earned rest with her mother in the hot summer of 1914, the project was well underway. The opening date was set for May 1915. But nothing could have prepared Edith for what was to happen over the next twelve months.

CHAPTER 9

DEDICATION AND DUTY

I WAS PASSING THROUGH BRUSSELS & YOUR DAUGHTER KEPT US
IN HIDING FROM THE GERMANS FOR 15 DAYS & TREATED US VERY
KINDLY.

(Lance corporal J. Doman of the 9th Lancers in a letter to Edith's
mother, 1915)

Edith was in England for the weeks before war with Germany
was declared. That summer the British people were far more
focused on Ireland, where plans for home-rule had stirred
tensions between Unionists and Nationalists. The assassination
of Austrian Archduke Franz Ferdinand and his wife in Bosnia's
capital, Sarajevo, on 28 June 1914 hadn't caused much of
a stir in sleepy Norfolk where Edith was on holiday visiting
her mother. Almost a month later, on 25 July, Norfolk's daily
newspaper, the *Eastern Daily Press* finally started to include
reports on the tensions which seemed far away in Eastern
Europe. No one seemed to realize that war would soon engulf
the continent. On Saturday 1 August, Sister Millicent White,
who had been left in charge of the nurses' training hospital,
sent an urgent telegram to Edith alerting her to the situation in
Belgium: war was imminent. The morning Bible reading that

day included Psalm 1 about righteous living, and Proverbs 27: 'Boast not thyself of to morrow; for thou knowest not what a day may bring forth' (verse 1, KJV) and the evening reading from the next chapter: '... the righteous are bold as a lion' (Proverbs 28:1, KJV).

Edith sought to live a godly life. She did not know what might happen next. But she did not hesitate when she heard of the impending war. She would not be persuaded to stay in England. 'At a time like this, I am more needed than ever,' she said.

Boldly, she set off for Belgium and arrived in Brussels in the early hours of Monday 3 August. Norah Symons, her near neighbour and friend, wrote in her diary: 'Miss Cavell at the clinique quite ready for wounded and Red Cross flags hung all over the house.' By 4 August, Britain was at war with Germany, with no guarantees that Belgian neutrality would be respected.

Edith's first task was to send the German nurses home. Most of her Dutch and English probationers also opted to leave. She took them herself to the Gare du Nord and waited with them until the last train out of Belgium took them across the Dutch border.

The Belgians were defiant and patriotic in the face of the enemy. Edith described the scene in an article she wrote for the *Nursing Mirror*:

> Flags were hung from end to end and no street,
> however mean, was without its stripes of yellow, red
> and black. Crowds assembled everywhere to talk over
> the prospects of a speedy peace, and the newspapers,
> published all day long, were sold in hundreds on every

street corner. The sun shone out and the glorious warm days of late summer were full of courage and anticipation.

Edith began preparations to receive the wounded in the nurses' training hospital and at the nearby St Gilles Hospital. Local people offered their help, giving mattresses and blankets. She expected to be busy tending injured soldiers and anticipated the worst as stories of burning, looting, and slaughter reached them.

But she wanted to allay her mother's fears. She wrote to her on 17 August:

> All is quiet at present. We live under martial law, and it is strange to be stopped in the street and have your papers and identity examined. If you should hear that the Germans are in Brussels, don't be alarmed. They will only walk through, as it is not a fortified town, and no fighting will take place in it. Besides we are living under the Red Cross. I should be very glad of some English papers as none have reached us since we left England. Two of our nurses arrived on Tuesday, having had a great deal of trouble to get through. My dearest love and Grace's. I will write whenever I can …

German army chief-of-staff Alfred von Schlieffen did not expect Belgium to resist. His plan was to march his troops straight into France. But the Belgian army was determined to stop the advancing enemy. The fortified Belgian city of Liège was the first to fall to the German Imperial Army. Hundreds of thousands died or were wounded in battles in that first month of war, as French and Belgian troops fought to hold their ground in Lorraine, Ardennes, Namur, Charleroi, and Mons where the British Expeditionary Force joined their French and Belgian allies.

Edith wrote a further letter on 19 August. It reads like a last will and testament:

My darling mother and family,

If you open this, it will be because that which we fear has now happened, and Brussels has fallen into the hands of the enemy. They are very near now and it is doubtful if the Allied armies can stop them. We are prepared for the worst.

I have given dear Gracie and the Sisters a chance to go home, but none of them will leave. I appreciate their courage and I want now to let the Jemmetts know that I did my best to send Gracie home, but she refused firmly to leave me – she is very quiet and brave.

I have nothing to leave but £160 in the Pension Fund, which has never been touched and is mine to leave. I wish mother to have it with my dearest love. It will supply the place of my little quarterly allowance to her.

If I can send my few jewels over will you divide them between Flor and Lil, and please give Mrs McDonnell my long gold chain which she gave me, and a keepsake to Marion Hall.

I shall think of you to the last, and you may be sure we shall do our duty here and die as women of our race should die.

> My dear, dear love to mother and Flor, Lil,
> Jack, Longworth and children; and also to Eveline
> McDonnell. God bless you and keep you safe.

On 20 August, the atmosphere in Brussels changed from defiance to compliance. The bright Belgian flags disappeared. Instead the black, white, and red German flags hung from the civic buildings marking the arrival of German troops and occupation. Edith's *Nursing Mirror* report took up the story as events unfolded:

> On August 13th we had no conception that soon, and for many long weary months, we were to be virtual prisoners in the gay city of Brussels ... We were full of enthusiasm for war, and full of confidence in the Allies ...
>
> After the period of high enthusiasm came the days of anxiety, growing keener hour by hour, when we heard Liège had fallen, that Namur followed, and that the enemy was coming on in irresistible force. There were sinister tales, too, of burnt and battered houses, of villages razed to the ground, of women and children murdered, of drunken soldiers and rapine [sic] and looting and annihilation. And still we hoped against hope. 'We wait for England' was on the lips of everyone, and till the very last we thought the English troops were between us and the invading army.
>
> In the afternoon [August 20] with much pomp and circumstance of war, the German troops marched into Brussels, and to the Town Hall, where the brave tricolor came down and the German stripes of black and white

and red took its place ... There were at least twenty thousand who entered the city that day and camped in it for the night ...

On August 21 many more troops came through; from our road we could see the long procession, and when the halt was called at mid-day and carts came up with supplies, some were too weary to eat and slept on the pavement of the street. We were divided between pity for these poor fellows, far from their country and their people, suffering the weariness and fatigue of an arduous campaign, and hate of a cruel and vindictive foe, bringing ruin and desolation on hundreds of happy homes and to a prosperous and peaceful land. Some of the Belgians spoke to the invaders in German, and found they were very vague as to their whereabouts, and imagined they were already in Paris; they were surprised to be speaking to Belgians and could not understand what quarrel they had with them. I saw several of the men pick up little children and give them chocolate or seat them on their horses ...

I am but a looker on after all, for it is not my country, whose soil is desecrated ... I can only feel the deep and tender pity of a friend within the gates, and observe with sympathy and admiration the high courage and self control of a people enduring a long and terrible agony ...

Needless to say Edith's mother was anxious about her daughter. Phone communication had been cut off, and letters were not being delivered by the postal service. As Edith watched the troops marching into Brussels on 21 August, Mrs Cavell wrote to her daughter and Grace.

> My darling Edith
>
> It is almost against hope that I am writing for news of you and Gracie – if at all possible do let me have a line or wire – no news is intolerable, one conjectures all sorts of things – my anxiety is terrible but I am afraid yours must be much worse, if you are both safe and well in the midst of all the horrors of war and invasion I shall be truly thankful – I pray constantly that God will grant you his loving protection ... I cannot write on any other topic my heart is full of one thing.
>
> My dearest love to you both dear child.
>
> Your loving Mother

Sixty miles south of Brussels in Dinant on 23 August, 674 men, women, and children were lined up in the city square and shot. Two days later, less than twenty miles from Brussels, the city of Louvin was set alight and citizens of all ages were executed as German troops sought to wipe out the city. But Brussels remained quiet.

On their way to Mons, the British sang upbeat songs such as 'Onward Christian Soldiers' and 'It's a Long Way to Tipperary'. Rumours of the 'Angels of Mons' lending supernatural assistance in battle were quick to spread as the Allied troops believed that God was on their side. A New Testament or prayer book was standard army kit, and prayer was a natural resort for troops who soon realized that the war would not be over by Christmas, as first expected. The German artillery bombardment on the British lines at Mons began at dawn on 23 August, and by the afternoon the British retreat had been ordered. There were 1,600 British casualties and double that number of German deaths.

On 30 August, Edith wrote again to her mother:

I know you must be in a state of great anxiety about us here in Brussels, but I hope you will receive the letter I sent through to Antwerp a day or two ago and that it will relieve your mind – a friend is going to Ninove tomorrow where he hears it is possible to wire and to post, he will take this & I hope you will get it shortly. If you do please send news to Flor & Lil also Mrs Jemmett, 'Elwick' Hillside Street, Hythe. They will be anxious tho' I hope news of the safety of Brussels has been published in the newspapers. I cannot give you details of things here, as this letter might fall into the wrong hands. We are almost without news of what is going on around us & tho' some filters thro' it is very unreliable. We would give anything for an English newspaper ... The wildest rumours are current – we know for certain there is fighting near at hand for we can hear the cannon & not far away the smoke can be seen with field glasses. We have a few German wounded in our hospital but here [the nurses' training hospital] there are none and the Allies are not brought to Brussels. There has been a terrible loss of life on both sides and destruction of towns and beautiful buildings that can never be rebuilt ... Gracie is not very well – one of her old attacks, brought on perhaps by the unsettled state of things – but this please do not tell the Jemmetts ...

In spite of the mounting casualty rate, it seems that Edith's earlier anxiety that she might never see her mother again had diminished, as she added: 'I am keeping a record for more peaceful times which will interest you later ... We go on quietly with our usual work...'

Already she was adapting to war, with its food shortages and limitations. She was finding ways to keep in contact with the outside world, sending letters with anyone she knew who was leaving Belgium, and sending her valuables back to England with Americans who were trying to cross the Channel.

Aiming to give her mother some peace of mind, she closed the letter: 'Do not fear for us, we are well out of the town as you know, and are not afraid.'

Her daily routine adapted to the fact that most of the probationers had gone, though there were still some Belgian nurses being trained. The training school sent their qualified nurses to hospitals such as St Gilles and to homes where they cared for private patients, but there were few patients being treated at rue de la Culture. The household included nurses Sister Millicent White, Sister Elisabeth Wilkins and Jacqueline van Til; six pupil nurses; Pauline Randall, Edith's goddaughter; Jose, a young Romanian who worked as a porter and handyman; plus housemaids, and linen room and laundry staff. Grace Jemmett was sometimes at the training hospital but also stayed with American friends in the city.

Edith's letter to her mother on 15 September still stressed how quiet the streets were:

> ... we have practically no work, life goes on as usual.
> There is plenty of food of which for a moment we
> were rather short and there is no reason to think we
> shall want for anything. The reason we can not write is
> because no trains are running to convey letters and the
> telegraphic communications are cut ...

However, she did add, 'There are a great many wounded in town ... our nurses are busy at work among them ... '

When they were not caring for the wounded, the nurses made clothes for the growing number of refugees who were arriving in the city. Food supplies had improved but the weather had turned cold, and Edith was worried about coal supplies for the winter as there were no trains running to make deliveries.

However, although Edith was at pains not to worry her mother, her neighbour, Ernest Symons, recorded more alarming news. He wrote in his diary:

> Sept. 16. Germans all over the place guarding avenue
> Hautpoint & rue de la Culture ... today they are
> examining all the covered carts & women's baskets to
> see if they are carrying clothes for the Belgian soldiers
> to escape from the hospitals and where they are
> imprisoned.

The Belgian and French resistance movements were growing and becoming more organized. Convents and castles had been commandeered by the Germans for use as hospitals, but priests, nuns, princes, and other patriotic Belgians were working against the invaders to help Allied soldiers to escape.

When Edith wrote to her sister Florence on 18 and 19 September, she explained that she had received a letter from their mother urging her to come home '... of course that is out of the question ...' was Edith's response. She was careful not to say too much, 'as our letters may fall into the wrong hands ...' And she still expected that she 'may later under different conditions have much work to do'.

It was an accurate prediction. British and French troops recovering from the battle at Mons took shelter in the 30,000 acre Forest of Mormal near the Franco-Belgian border. Some of those injured at Mons had found their way to the nearby castle of Bellignies, home of Prince Reginald de Croy and his sister, Princess Marie. There the princess nursed them back to health alongside German casualties. When twenty-two German officers arrived at the castle on 25 August, one insisted on checking that the British were genuinely wounded by removing their bandages. The German officers continued to be suspicious when they were served dinner; the de Croys had to taste every dish served to prove it was not poisoned. Princess Marie's response was blunt and reminiscent of Edith's motivation: 'I am here to save life, not to take it.'

But the German distrust of the de Croys was well-founded. As well as caring for injured Allied soldiers, the de Croys were key to the resistance movement. They hid escaping Allied troops in a disused staircase in the castle tower. They arranged to feed fugitives in the forest, providing them with clothes, and arranging their safe passage out of occupied Belgium.

Princess Marie also used her illegally concealed camera to provide photographs for forged passports, developing the photos herself.

The de Croys were supported by two young women who scoured the forest looking for hidden Allied soldiers who needed help to escape across the border into neutral Holland. Princess Marie described the girls in her diary: 'One was Mlle Moriamé, the brewer's sister (he is fighting) and the other is her neighbour, Mlle Louise Thuliez, a schoolmistress from Lille, who was spending her holidays with relations in the village when war broke out.'

The duo, whom Princess Marie dubbed the 'girl guides', hid injured English soldiers in Henriette Moriamé's house, even though British soldiers and the Belgians who concealed them were being shot when found. Soon notices were posted everywhere to say that any inhabitants harbouring French or Allied soldiers would face the death penalty. But Henriette, Louise, and their co-conspirators continued to rescue Allied soldiers trapped behind enemy lines, finding safe houses for them until they could help them escape.

Rowland Ryder met Louise Thuliez years later in 1966 in her flat in Paris to record first-hand her recollections about the exploits of these courageous women. He described them as 'devout Christians', along with another accomplice, Countess Jeanne de Belleville of Montignies-sur-Roc near Bellignies. The countess looked after 400 wounded English soldiers in the convent at Audregnies after the Battle of Mons. Louise Thuliez and the countess shared a cell on the last night of Edith's life and were reading their prayer books as the execution was carried out.

A third base for escaping troops was the convent hospital at Wihéries, which had been turned into a makeshift hospital for Allied and German troops. Colonel Dudley Boger and Sergeant Frederick Meachin who had been injured at Mons were two of the British soldiers treated there by Dr Valentin van Hassel.

As soon as Boger and Meachin were fit to travel, they made their escape to avoid being sent to an internment camp. Dr van Hassel's son-in-law, Albert Libiez, a lawyer, hid them in his home until Boger had grown a beard. Boger then dressed in typically Belgian clothes, with a black hat and floppy tie, and Meachin put shoulder pads under peasants' overalls to make him look like a hunchback. In late October 1914, two nuns guided them to a second convent where they were met by Herman Capiau, a local mining engineer. He took them on to Brussels.

Once they arrived in the city, Capiau contacted Marie Depage, whose husband had established the nursing school, to find lodgings for the two stranded English soldiers. Almost as an afterthought, she directed them to Edith Cavell, who took them in without hesitation. Edith's role in the Belgian resistance movement had begun.

Boger and Meachin stayed at the training hospital for nearly three weeks while Boger's wounds were treated and healed. Before setting off on the final stage of their escape, Boger handed his report for the War Office to Sister Millicent White. After he left the training hospital, Colonel Boger was arrested and sent to an internment camp as a prisoner of war, but Meachin made it back to England. Initially he was arrested as a suspected deserter, but eventually he received the Distinguished Conduct Medal (DCM) for 'gallantry in the field'.

In a chatty letter home about this time, Edith wrote:

> All is quiet at present and life goes on much as usual
> except that there is very little work either for us or for
> anybody else, you would think every day a Sunday – so
> few shops and houses open and so many people walking
> about with nothing to do. The streets are strangely quiet
> with no motors, it makes it much easier and pleasanter
> getting about, you would certainly prefer it. We have
> the trams as usual, but at night they may not go through
> certain parts of the town … There are fewer lights too
> in the evening in the streets some of which are as dark
> as in the middle ages, all the houses shuttered and the
> shops shut. It looks very gloomy and strange. There is
> very little coal … Butter is 6d. a lb dearer at the very
> cheapest … Meat has gone up in price & milk & eggs
> are rather scarce but fruit & vegetables are cheap –
> especially grapes. Most beautiful ones can be bought
> for 3d or 4d per lb. … We have to practise economy as
> so little money is coming in at present …

She also passed on news of Grace, who had been ill in bed for six weeks. Her neighbours, the Symonses, had returned to England, as had the English clergyman who pastored the Chapelle de la Résurrection, which had closed.

'We have to go to Christ Church where there is a new chaplain', she wrote. The chaplain, Revd Stirling Gahan, was to become a friend, and his was to be the last English voice Edith heard before her execution.

On 19 October, Edith wrote again to her mother:

Everything goes on as usual, tho' all around the unusual
is happening … We are short of nothing at present,
tho' there is a scarcity in the poor quarters & will be
much misery all through the winter – we are engaged
in making up the stuff we can get into garments for the
children of the refugees and the other poor. Coal is
scarce but we hope that supplies will soon come in as a
means of transit has been opened. I have much to tell
you later on but cannot write it now …

In the letter, she asked her mother to keep the envelopes from
her correspondence

so that we can see by what means they arrive when
I return home … Think of us going steadily on with
our work here & the hospital & living from day to day
cheerfully & with good hope for the future …

The October letter was delivered by an Englishman, Giles
Hibbard, who posted it from London. Many of the English
residents of Brussels were returning to Britain.

Another newsy letter followed on 8 November, thanking
her mother for

the little blue woollen jacket you gave me [which]
has been a great comfort. I wear it every day when I
am sitting over accounts or writing. Many people are
without bread, tho' other foods hold out. We have given
it up for dinner and supper, but have an allowance for
other meals – it is often almost black and heavy but
quite eatable …

She described plans for a children's Christmas party. The nurses were dressing dolls as well as making clothes for refugee children. 'We are hoping to make a Xmas tree for the poor children this year instead of for ourselves – there are twelve dolls dressed already and a good many clothes made.' Edith also described long walks with Jackie, her adopted stray dog, and a bunch of chrysanthemums on her table 'nearly as big as soup plates' in a vase made from an empty shell case. In a letter to her sister Lilian she said,

> We have quickly accommodated ourselves to very
> altered circumstances and have learned to live in
> a modern 'Middle Ages'; no trains, no motors, no
> bicycles, no post, no telephone, no telegraph, very
> few street lights, sometimes a scarcity of bread and a
> general limit to ease and comfort; it is wonderful how
> soon such things cease to be a necessity and are scarcely
> missed ... Sometimes we hear the cannon for days
> altogether and sometimes not at all and then we miss
> it. Poverty is beginning to be felt, the people are selling
> their furniture and tho' the Communes supply them
> with some soup and bread it is only enough to keep
> body and soul together.

By 22 November, there was thick snow on the ground and it was bitterly cold in Brussels. Edith wrote: 'All Englishmen of a certain age have been taken prisoner and we are very closely surrounded...' and more cryptically:

> We have had some interesting work but are quiet again
> now. Our people who left last week must have arrived
> safely as they have not returned – if so you will have
> sent £2 for me to Miss Millicent White c/o Dr White
> whose address you know; it is the rest of her salary
> which I owe her.

Sister White had escaped to Antwerp on a barge, carrying Colonel Boger's dispatches for the War Office wrapped in bandages around her leg. She was stopped and searched, but reached England safely with these vital reports.

Soon, news of Edith's role in arranging the escape of the two English soldiers reached the de Croys. The prince visited Edith to explain the plight of the soldiers hiding in the forest and in nearby villages. Many needed treatment for battle wounds. All needed a place to hide on their way to the Dutch border. Edith sealed her fate when she agreed to help.

From the start of November, each week a wounded French soldier who had been treated by one of the training hospital's surgeons in a field hospital arrived at rue de la Culture, where they stayed for a couple of days until Edith found a guide to take them across the Dutch frontier. The password for the escapees was 'Yorc' – Croy, spelt backwards. Edith cared for the soldiers as patients with fictitious operations recorded in her training hospital records. Always careful to protect her nurses, Edith took full responsibility for the soldiers in their care, but they were not easy to keep under control. Two even joined the Christmas party, which Edith and the nurses held for about thirty refugee children.

After the Battle of Mons, Sergeant Jesse Tunmore and Private

White were the sole survivors of their platoon, which was part of the Norfolk regiment. They too were treated at the convent at Wihéries, and Tunmore made his escape with Private Lewis of the Cheshire regiment, this time helped by a miner called August Joly, 'girl guide' Louise Thuliez's brother-in-law. He gave them civilian clothes and took them to the training hospital. Initially wary, Edith soon discovered Tunmore was Norfolk-born when he recognized a painting of Norwich Cathedral on her office wall. Tunmore and Lewis spent Christmas 1914 in Edith's care. Their first escape attempt in a cart failed as their paperwork was out of date, so they returned to Edith who helped them to make a successful getaway on foot. Tunmore never forgot Edith Cavell, who had played such a significant role in his life. When Edith's body was finally repatriated, Tunmore was one of the pall-bearers when she was laid to rest in Norwich.

Tunmore told biographer A. E. Clark-Kennedy Edith helped them to escape on foot, avoiding the direct route to Antwerp:

> She herself at dawn one morning guided me and Pte Lewis through the streets of Brussels on to the Louvain Road. No one else of her staff did anything like this. I know that for certain. It was she herself, too, who took the photos for certificates of identity for us, and she herself went to the necessary department and fetched back the identity cards. She also gave us food and money to use for bribing and travelling by railway.

When Christmas came and troops from both sides stopped fighting for the remarkable Christmas truce of 1914, Edith and the nurses also broke with their routine to celebrate Jesus' birth. There was roast beef and a plum pudding made to Mrs Cavell's recipe for the nurses. There were the thirty children who received their gifts, and a special guest, Revd Stirling Gahan, the only English-speaking clergyman left in Brussels, who said later,

> I joined the party in the late hours of the afternoon, and found a good many friends there, with a number of unknown Belgian folk. Nurse Cavell moved pleasantly among her guests, and there, to our great amusement and delight, were a couple of British 'Tommies'! How we gripped hands! ... There was a spice of danger in it, but that was all, and we did not think of any special risk for the Matron. There was more ground for hope than fear!

Tunmore remembered Edith chatting with the soldiers hidden at the training hospital and wishing them a merry Christmas. He described her as 'slim, quiet, kind in every way – and clever'. Once he was back in England he wrote on 20 January 1915 to Edith's mother:

> I am writing to say that your daughter the Matron of the Nurses' School in Brussels, Belgium, is quite well. I am a soldier of the 1st Norfolk Regiment & she has done a lot for helping me to escape over the frontier to Holland ... I cannot express enough thanks for all she done for me, she worked very hard for us indeed ... I spent Xmas & the New Year with your daughter.

After returning home, Tunmore spent some time in hospital straightjacketed and suffering from 'acute mania'. But when he recovered, he wrote again to Mrs Cavell who replied, sending him 'the best of earthly blessings' adding,

> I hope you feel thankful to God for His great mercy ...
> there is much distress which Miss Cavell and her nurses
> do their utmost to relieve – May God bless her and
> bring her home in peace that I may see her again. Life
> with me is uncertain as I am in my 81st year.

Edith was scrupulously honest, and kept accounts of all she spent caring for both patients and escapees. Later, when the danger of being discovered became too great, she had to destroy these records, and worried that when the war ended she would not be able to give a proper account for the money spent. Princess Marie de Croy assured her that she would vouch for her honesty to the training hospital committee. But the missing accounts did not escape the attention of a visiting German officer, who noticed that her records had not been kept up to date.

As more and more escaping soldiers passed through the training hospital, Edith faced growing risks. In January 1915, she took in two English soldiers, Lance corporal J. Doman of the 9th Lancers, and Corporal P. Chapman of the Cheshires. They had a narrow escape when German officials arrived unannounced; Doman jumped into bed with his boots still on. Fortunately, Edith insisted that all the wards were cleaned with beds ready for 'patients' at a moment's notice.

A couple of days later, Edith took Doman and Chapman

to rendezvous with their guide at a small café. Lance corporal Doman told the story himself in his correspondence with Rowland Ryder:

> Having ordered three beers, Miss C. ... placed half
> of a card on one of the tables. Some minutes later
> a man entered, and upon noticing the half card on
> the table, placed a corresponding half beside it. This
> manner of procedure must have been arranged by
> correspondence, as the guide was unknown to Miss
> C. ... Just outside the café there was a kind of outpost
> of Germans who appeared to be billeted in the next
> building ... After wishing us good-bye, Miss C. ... left
> us in charge of the guide, who conducted us to a small
> village south of Antwerp.

The men made it back to Britain and Doman wrote to Mrs Cavell:

> I am a wounded soldier and was taken prisoner in
> Belgium where I escaped from. I was passing through
> Brussels & your daughter kept us in hiding from the
> Germans for 15 days & treated us very kindly. She
> got us a guide to bring us through [to] Holland & we
> arrived in England quite safe.

Mrs Cavell seems to have picked up from the letter that Edith was in danger and must have written to Doman. A few weeks later in mid-February, Doman wrote:

> Referring to it being risky for her well I don't think she
> has much to fear as when the Germans are about the

English do not remain in her house, but go out and hide
in the town, & I do not think she will have any more
prisoners there as we were the last two who were left ... I
think that when the war is over she will be highly praised
and well rewarded for the good work she has done.

Private Arthur Wood, another fugitive who passed through the
training hospital, wrote to Mrs Cavell after Edith's death:

... she treated me as my own Mother would have done
and proved herself to be the very best friend I ever had.
I am not the only English soldier that your daughter
befriended, there are four more in my own regiment
besides the men of other Regiments she helped.

One of those men at the training hospital at the same time as
Private Wood was Frank Holmes from Norfolk. His home in
Norwich was in easy walking distance of Mrs Cavell's house.
Edith gave him her Bible and a letter for her mother, which
Frank delivered, but it would seem that Mrs Cavell was too
wary of potential spies who might betray her daughter, so her
maid turned Frank away.

By March 1915, the resistance movement had become well
established and even had its own newspaper, *La Libre Belgique.*
This particularly angered General von Bissing, the German
military governor in occupied Belgium. On seven occasions, a
resistance fighter disguised as a German officer stole documents
from von Bissing's private office safe, leaving behind a copy of
La Libre Belgique. With hindsight such taunts seem ill-advised
and may well have fuelled German anger, leading to the death
of Philippe Baucq, executed on the same morning as Edith.

Philippe Baucq, a Brussels-born architect, managed the distribution of 25,000 copies of *La Libre Belgique* on average five times a month. Under the pseudonym Monsieur Fromage, Baucq spied for the Allies by sending them his sketches of the zeppelin hangars. He also worked out many of the escape routes for Allied soldiers.

Between February and July 1915, Edith hid an estimated 170 soldiers at the training hospital while she arranged for guides to accompany them to the Dutch border. But the Germans were watching activities at rue de la Culture. A house on the other side of the road was used to billet German troops, and at night they could be seen through the windows playing cards and drinking.

As more and more fugitives turned to Edith for help, careless risks were taken. One escapee, Harry Beaumont, told Rowland Ryder that there were about eighteen soldiers hidden in a room at the top of Edith's house when he was there. Soldiers routinely went out in the evening. One night a group returned drunk, singing 'It's a Long Way to Tipperary' at the tops of their voices as they made their way back along rue de la Culture. The next morning they were moved quickly to other safe houses.

Edith's letters home were also becoming less discreet. On 1 March she wrote to her cousin Eddy, saying, 'I am helping in ways I may not describe to you now...' and she asked for his assistance to collect money for the poor in Brussels. Ten days later in a letter to her mother she explained '... we are policed by the enemy and people are arrested often without warning'. She knew they were being watched: 'An immense zeppelin passed over the plain and our house yesterday evening seeming just to clear the roof.' Also, she had a German maid called Marie who had remained when the other German residents of Brussels left at the outbreak of war. Edith told her mother, 'Marie has been giving me a good deal of trouble. I expect I shall have to send her away one of these days, but must wait in prudence, till after the war.' She even asked if her mother had heard from Doman and Chapman who had stayed at the training hospital in January 1915.

Alongside the resistance work, Edith was overseeing progress on the new premises for the nursing school, though plans to open on 1 May 1915 had been shelved. Dr Depage was serving with the Belgian army and his wife, Marie, had gone to America to raise funds for Belgium, but the aim was still to open the new, state-of-the-art training hospital as soon as possible, war or no war.

But German suspicions over activities in the nurses' training hospital were growing. There were an estimated 6,000 spies in Brussels at the time. Edith noticed strange workmen in the street whose work appeared to achieve nothing, and she suspected that some of those who claimed to be fugitives were in fact in the pay of the Germans. It would not be long before the resistance network was infiltrated. Edith was putting her life on the line.

CHAPTER 10

BETRAYAL

... WE CANNOT STOP BECAUSE IF A SINGLE ONE OF THESE MEN
WERE TAKEN AND SHOT, THAT WOULD BE OUR FAULT.

(Edith Cavell, 1915)

Edith kept a secret diary recording her experiences in occupied Belgium. Only a few pages have survived as they were sewn into a cushion, only coming to light in the 1940s. The pages made the cushion lumpy, but before it was thrown away it was opened to reveal Edith's secret diary for April 1915. Rowland Ryder speculated that she had used a microscope to write it as her distinctive script is so small. She described events and people vividly and in far more detail than her letters. She knew she was in danger.

On 27 April she wrote:

> ... The frontier has been absolutely impassable the last few days G[ermany] and H[olland] have been on the verge of war ... The Dutch refused to allow anyone to cross and had massed their troops & laid mines all along from Maastricht to Antwerp, a sentinel on the D[utch] side was posted every 15 metres & all the young men who had left to try & cross were stuck or

came back – 5 of ours were heard of at Herrenthall
yesterday morning & the guide left to bring them back.
Last night great numbers of G[erman] wounded passed
thro' the city; the Gare de Schaerbeck was cleared of
the public to let them thro' – all the Dutch newspapers
were burned at the G. du Midi. None from France or
Eng. have come through for some days ...

As well as abbreviating country names to initials, she used
noms de guerre for her fellow resistance fighters. Philippe Baucq
was Monsieur Fromage or M. Fr. She was chronicling events
from her unique perspective as an English nurse in occupied
territory at a pivotal moment in European history. Aware of the
danger she was in, she wrote about rumours and speculated
about German intentions. She recorded news of air raids and
of ammunitions depots which had been destroyed. And she
detailed the events which would eventually lead to her arrest.
'M. Fr brought me word from the town authorities that the
house is watched and several attempts I think have been made
to catch me...' she wrote. '... several suspicious persons have
been to ask for help to leave the country either in the form of
money, lodging or guides. People have been taken in this way
several times...'

A doctor had been arrested when caught carrying a letter
to post in Holland. '... he also had one for me,' she wrote, 'but
as yet I have heard nothing of this.' The Countess d'Ursel had
been arrested after carrying information in her garter for the
resistance movement. But, regardless of the dangers she faced,
Edith continued finding safe houses for escaping Allied soldiers
and guides to take them safely out of Belgium.

Meal times at the nurses' training hospital included an eclectic mix of guests, according to Edith's diary. One of the guides with the *nom de guerre*, Victor Gilles, who 'dines & sups here occasionally', was a country postman who had helped with ambulance services at the Battle of Mons. He had made the acquaintance of Miss Nellie Hozier, one of Winston Churchill's relatives, who sent him to England to take her letters to Churchill, who was First Lord of the Admiralty. The postman and the prime minister-to-be met in the library at Admiralty House and Churchill took him to see his wife and newborn baby, Sarah Churchill, who had been born on 7 October 1914.

Other training hospital guests included the Baroness de Cromburgghe, one of the Belgian nobility, who came to tea with one of Edith's nurses, Sister Kathleen Cambridge. Sister Cambridge had been caring for a patient in Mons when war was declared. They told Edith about the wounded soldiers the Baroness had cared for in her home. More news came from 'M. Victor ... a tradesman of 60 or thereabouts with a pale & puffy face, bald-headed, fat & short. He has a benevolent smile & spends his days in going from place to place to look after our guests'.

Charles Venderlinden, one of the guides for the escapees, is described in great detail in Edith's diary, which was dated '31 Ap[ril] 1915' even though there is no such date in the calendar; an unusual mistake for someone normally so meticulous. She wrote,

> This boy of 23 is one of a family of 9 sons, all strong and fighters. 3 are colonial volunteers & 1 is in the reg. army, 2 little ones are dying to pass the frontier

and enlist. Charles says he will take them if it becomes
easier. This fellow is a fine type – about 5ft 6 or 7
slightly made but very strong and muscular.

Charles was a boxer and had been blinded in one eye in a
fight. He told Edith how to break a man's neck... 'to catch a
man's head under the arm & "crack" his neck or to give him a
back-handed blow and destroy the trachea or larynx'. He was
a poacher in peacetime and had explained to Edith how he
set the traps so that he and his three friends could catch up to
thirty hares in two or three days.

Edith was aware of his weaknesses:

He is nearly always sober but when on the drink will
be drunk for 10 days on the stretch. He & his brothers,
men equally strong and pugilistic, would fight at times,
but when they entered a café together no one dare say a
word to any of them.

However, she evidently respected this young man who, she
wrote,

has travelled far oftener on foot than otherwise &
has many trades to which he can turn his hand. He is
extremely intelligent & has a good memory. He has
ideas of justice & straight dealing & is very anxious to
repay any money given him ...

Edith was equally concerned to be honest in her dealings and
noticed such qualities in others.

> He boasts in the most open manner & enjoys to talk
> of himself & his prowess. Withal he is, at least here, a
> gentleman and well-behaved in the house & gives us no
> trouble, also his conversation is clean & quite pleasing
> ... He is very scornful over the men with no pluck &
> has grand contempt for the G[erman]s ... He can swim
> & walk great distances, also knows how to pass a leisure
> day sound asleep on our garden grass ... He wears his
> trousers tied in at the ankle & under the tie places his
> letters – or ours.

She knew that by guiding escaping soldiers to the border he was putting his life in danger: 'He will be caught one day & if so will be shot but he will make a first class bid for life and freedom', she wrote. Edith knew the penalty awaiting those who helped Allied troops to freedom, and she knew she was under surveillance: 'Today a great airship passed low over the houses & displayed the No. 179 & was plainly visible as also the men in the car ... There are now 2 captive balloons which survey the city from different angles.' Tethered balloons with cameras attached were used to take aerial photographs.

She tried to be careful. The training hospital often cared for patients who had been injured in industrial accidents. People were coming and going throughout the day, making it easier to hide the arrival of escapees in their various disguises. One visitor to the training hospital, Raoul de Roy, who wanted to escape across the frontier, told Rowland Ryder that he was cross-examined closely by two guides before he was given a rendezvous point. But the net was closing in. The German political police, the *Geheime Politische Polizei*, known to the

Belgians as 'the Berlin Vampires', were compiling a dossier on the resistance activities.

Edith was always on the lookout, ready to respond if the secret police visited the training hospital. She hid Charlie Scott, a Norfolk-born soldier, in a barrel one night when the Germans sprang a surprise search on them. Once he was inside the barrel, she tipped apples on top of him so he would not be found. But in May 1915, Edith told fellow resistance fighter Countess Jeanne de Belleville 'tell the helpers not to send any more men here for the present, as my situation is becoming more and more strained every day'.

May began with a severe blow for the little resistance group. Edith's friend Madame Depage, the wife of the Belgian doctor who started the school, was drowned. She was on board the *Luisitania* on her way back from fundraising in America, when the liner was sunk by a German U-boat: 1,198 of the 1,959 people on board were lost at sea.

But efforts to support the Allies continued, with more and more soldiers passing through the training hospital. Not far from rue de la Culture, the *Geheime Politische Polizei* had identified Edith Cavell as a suspect. This local branch of the secret police was run by Lieutenant Bergan with Henri Pinkhoff and Otto Mayer under his command. Pinkhoff was determined to catch Edith and have her executed. Otto Mayer was sent to search the training hospital to uncover the necessary evidence.

Edith was out on a regular visit to review progress on the new school building when he arrived. Nurse Elisabeth Wilkins told Rowland Ryder that there were two French and two Belgian soldiers in one of the wards that day. From the hospital stairs she saw a strange man in the hall wearing a bedraggled mackintosh. 'Have you any more?' he asked her. Assuming he was asking for more nurses, she replied 'No.'

'What, no more Tommies?' came the quick retort. The stranger then turned back the lapel of his coat to show her his badge: Otto Mayer, *Geheime Politische Polizei*. It was the worst moment of her life, Elisabeth told Ryder. Thinking on her feet, she then added, 'If you don't believe me you had better come into my own room, and you can search my desk if you want to.'

After searching her room, he asked to see the wards. The first was full of genuine patients and, as they walked in, Elisabeth indicated to the nurse on duty that their visitor was German. As Mayer checked the ward, the nurse alerted the four hidden soldiers so they could make their escape, with the help of Jose the handyman. But Elisabeth knew that Edith's records were in her office. While Mayer looked at the authentic patients' records, Elisabeth made an excuse, went straight to Edith's rooms and gathered up the incriminating paperwork. She then jammed it into the cistern in the nearest toilet. By the time Mayer came to search Edith's office, the evidence was out of sight.

But Elisabeth's ordeal was not over. The secret police were back within the month to search again. This time Elisabeth was arrested and taken to police headquarters and held for questioning for three hours. She denied knowing anything about soldiers on the run and was released.

From mid-June onwards the training hospital was raided almost every week. Edith burned most of her records, on one occasion throwing papers into the grate and pouring alcohol on them to set them alight before the approaching German visitor opened her office door. She hid some records under the floor in a bistro nearby, but all that survived were the letters sent back to England and the few 'cushion diary' pages. She had told one of her 'guests' that she was keeping a photo album of all the soldiers who passed through the training hospital, but it was never found.

Princess Marie de Croy wrote in her memoirs that she visited Edith to tell her the castle at Bellignies had been searched. Edith told her, 'I wish you hadn't come; I am evidently suspect. Look at those men clearing the square in front; they have been there for several days and are scarcely working at all. They must be set to watch the house.'

But when Princess Marie explained that more escaping soldiers were in hiding and waiting to cross the border, Edith was firm: 'Then we cannot stop because if a single one of these men were taken and shot, that would be our fault.'

They agreed to help the men, hiding them in their network of safe houses. The training hospital was no longer an adequate hiding place.

As the princess left the hospital, Edith gave her a tried and tested route to avoid being followed. The princess said:

> I was to go to the end of the road where a shop window reflected the street behind me, and stand looking in this window for a moment. I must then quickly turn down the road on the left to where another shop, if I remember rightly a pâtisserie this time, was in front of the spot where the tram stopped. I was to stand hesitating as though I was to enter this shop until I heard the bell announce that a tram was going to start, and turn and jump on the tram as it was moving off,

> not minding in which direction it went. These different
> manoeuvres were pretty sure to throw anybody who
> might have followed me off the track, and I carried
> them out exactly.

Tension was mounting. Dr Marcel Detry, one of the surgeons, said Edith was 'jumpy' in the operating theatre, and would pull the curtain aside to look up the street when she heard anything unusual.

When Sister Wilkins went with Edith to inspect developments at the new building, Edith explained in detail where everything should go and how they should operate once the new school was open. It was as if she knew she would never see the building used, Elisabeth said later.

On 14 June, Edith wrote to home. It was to be the last letter to her mother that reached England.

> My darling Mother
>
> Very many happy returns of your birthday & my best
> love & good wishes – I have always made a point of
> being at home for July 6, but this year it will not be
> possible, even if one could leave the country to return
> takes a long while for I heard England expects 2 months
> notice before giving a passport. It is still a long while
> to your birthday but I am not sure of having another
> occasion of sending & letters probably take a long while
> to arrive ...

Edith hadn't received any of the letters her mother had written since 24 January. News had reached her that Mrs Cavell was well, but in this letter Edith wrote,

> Do not forget if anything very serious should happen
> you could probably send me a message thro' the
> American Ambassador in London. (not a letter) All
> is quiet here as usual. We are only a small number so
> many being at the front nursing the Belgian soldiers –
> but we also have less work for no one can think about
> being ill at present.

Keen to keep her mother up to date with progress on the building project she explained,

> Our new school is still unfinished and I see no prospect
> of moving in – the little garden in front flourishes but
> the ground at the back cannot be planted as it is still
> encumbered with bricks and rubbish.'

She was concerned about finance and asked if Grace's father, Mr Jemmett, had sent 'the £50 I asked for thro' the Embassy if not I hope he will do so at once – as we are needing money. We have not heard a word either from him or Mrs J. for many months.' Still hopeful that they would see each other this side of eternity, she added, 'I should like to say more but leave all the interesting things till I see you again.'

Events took a turn for the worse when George Gaston Quien arrived at the training hospital. He claimed to be an injured French officer. In fact, he was a conman who had been in prison for theft when war broke out. Dubbed the 'lamp-post' as he was six foot five inches tall, he was a ladies' man and soon started flattering the kitchen maid and nurses. Edith and Elisabeth Wilkins had their suspicions about him but, always the professional, Edith gave him the same care she gave all her patients and treated his injured foot. Quien used his convalescence at the training hospital to chat to the staff, finding out as much as he could about their activities. Edith arranged his escape at the end of June, but she had not seen the last of him.

It was a hot summer. As well as occasional thunder, Edith and the nurses could hear the sound of bombing raids on the Zeppelin sheds to the east of Brussels. On 7 June 1915, Flight Sub-Lieutenant Reginald Warneford from England attacked and completely destroyed a Zeppelin in mid-air. He was awarded the Victoria Cross for his actions. The citation in the *London Gazette* read:

> This brilliant achievement was accomplished after chasing the Zeppelin from the coast of Flanders to Ghent, where he succeeded in dropping his bombs on to it from a height of only one or two hundred feet. One of these bombs caused a terrific explosion which set the Zeppelin on fire from end to end, but at the same time overturned his Aeroplane and stopped the engine.

Warneford had to land behind enemy lines to repair the plane, but was soon back in the air and flying home. Edith's letter to her mother mentioned the daring escapade. 'We were awakened by the noise and saw the smoke & flame…'

Raids on the Zeppelin hangars stoked German fury against the English and Belgians. For Lieutenant Bergan, Henri Pinkhoff, and Otto Mayer, the enemy was embodied in Edith Cavell and Philippe Baucq, whom they saw as the ringleaders of a significant resistance movement in Brussels. Edith had helped fugitive soldiers to escape. Baucq had drawn maps revealing the sites of the Zeppelin hangars and had distributed thousands of copies of the underground newspaper *La Libre Belgique.*

Although she was the 'enemy', Edith still won the hearts of some of the spies sent to betray her. In July, Armand Jeannes stayed at the training hospital under the name of Jacoby. When he left, they found a note he had written to say he could not act against people who had been so kind to him. His sympathies were short-lived, however. He was responsible for the arrests of Marie Claire Libiez and Herman Capiau, who stood trial with Edith three months later.

Belgian independence day 'celebrations' added further fuel to German fury on 21 July. Festivities and parades had been banned, so the Belgians decided to mark their national day with mourning focused on a Solemn High Mass at the city's cathedral. As the Mass ended, the organist began to play the Belgian national anthem with its triumphant declaration: '*Le Roi, la Loi, la Liberté!*' (The King, the Law, and Liberty!). It was sung softly at first, but by the fifth rendition they were shouting at the tops of their voices. The next edition of *La Libre Belgique* carried a full report on the day's events. Ten days later, the arrests began.

The secret police had been compiling their evidence on thirty-five suspects, including Edith Cavell and Philippe Baucq. These resistance fighters could sense that time was short. On 27 July, Baucq went to his favourite café to play cards with his friends. As he left his parting words were: 'I don't think that you will see me again in here.'

Back home in England, Mrs Cavell was sent a letter dated 28 July 1915 from Ruth de Borchgrave, a member of the training hospital ladies' committee who was in England.

I have had a message from Brussels asking me to write
to tell you not to speak to any one of your daughter
there. Also to warn you against a certain man – reddish
face and fair short military moustache, real Cockney
accent, who says he has a flower shop in Forest Hill,
London.

I am sending this letter through the Chief Constable
of Norwich whom I have asked to take note of its
contents.

Your daughter is an old friend of mine and [I] would
gladly help her in any way.

On 29 July, Philippe Baucq took his elder daughter for a walk
and explained that he might soon be arrested. If so, she should
claim ignorance about any of his activities.

That same day Quien returned to the training hospital. He
had a bouquet of flowers for Edith and another tall story. This
time he claimed to be working for French intelligence. Edith
did not allow him to stay, and Elisabeth Wilkins saw him talking
to German sympathizers shortly afterwards.

Another two days passed, and Quien was seen near Philippe
Baucq's house. That night, at 10.30 p.m. on 31 July, Baucq and
Louise Thuliez were arrested. When the police searched his
house, they found 4,000 copies of issue thirty-seven of *La
Libre Belgique* ready for distribution. Louise had been visiting
Philippe after leaving six fugitives at a safe house. She tried to
hide her handbag behind a bath when the police arrived, but
it was found. In it was her coded address book, a false identity
card, and a receipt for 'lodging six men for four days' which had
been paid only a few hours earlier.

One of the safe houses was run by Ada Bodart. Her son Philippe, who was just fourteen, was also arrested at Baucq's house. When Prince Reginald de Croy heard of the arrests, he went to warn Ada Bodart. She then offered to pass on the news to the rest of the resistance fighters. But the police were waiting to catch the prince and arrested Ada instead.

Edith's goddaughter Pauline Randall was drawn into the plot on 2 August. Quien spotted her out walking with the cook's daughter from the training hospital and invited them for a drink. Keeping up his flirtatious banter, he asked if Edith could help get his friend out of Belgium. Later evidence suggests that Pauline was persuaded to pass on gossip which was used to secure Edith's conviction.

On 4 August, a German inspector arrived at the training hospital and took up residence in one of the reception rooms. The following afternoon, Thursday 5 August, Pinkhoff and Mayer arrived, ranting and raving, searching the building and ransacking Edith's office.

Finally Edith was arrested, together with Elisabeth Wilkins. The pretext for taking them into custody was a letter Pinkhoff and Mayer found from England with the American consulate's stamp on the back. It was illegal for the consulate to deliver correspondence for the 'enemy'. They were driven to police headquarters for questioning. Elisabeth was released. Edith was not. She was now a prisoner of the German political police, facing charges of treason.

CHAPTER 11

SENTENCED TO DEATH

… IT IS A GOOD THING SOMETIMES TO STOP AND LOOK BACK
UPON THE PATH WE HAVE TRAVELLED TO TAKE STOCK OF OUR
PROGRESS AND THE MISTAKES WE HAVE MADE …

(Edith Cavell, in a letter written to her nurses the night before
she died)

Lieutenant Bergan, head of espionage in Brussels, was waiting for Edith Cavell and Elisabeth Wilkins at police headquarters. Otto Mayer interrogated Elisabeth, telling her that Quien had provided the necessary evidence against the nurses. She told them that she knew nothing. Later she wrote: 'I never knew why they released me but at eight that night I was told that I might go.'

Edith was not so fortunate. After initial questioning, she was sent to the communal women's cell. On 6 August she wrote to Grace:

My dearest Gracie,

Let's hope you are not worrying about me – tell
everybody that I am quite all right here. I suppose from
what I hear that I shall be questioned one of these days

> and when they have all they desire I shall know what
> they mean to do with me. We are numerous here and
> there is no chance of being lonely. We can buy food at
> the canteen, but I should be glad to have one of your
> red blankets, a serviette, cup, fork, spoon, and plate.
> Not best ones – also two towels and my toothbrush. In
> a day or two some clean linen. I'm afraid you will not be
> able to come to see me at present – but you can write,
> only your letters will be read.

She also asked if Sister Wilkins was free and told them to continue with the move to the new building. 'If Sister is there, she will know how to arrange everything.'

Optimistic that she would soon be free, she added, 'If Jackie is sad, tell him I will be back soon.' She also asked for a book and some embroidery to while away the long hours, and some nail scissors. The Imperial War Museum has a small, white lace square Edith completed while in prison. She ended the letter asking for news of the hospital laundress who had been unwell and added,

> There is a small child of three or four here with her
> mother; she looks pale and pinched for want of air,
> though she is allowed out a while every day.
>
> I will write again when there is anything to tell.
> Don't – don't worry. We must hope for the best. Tell
> them all to go on as usual.

Edith was transferred to cell twenty-three in St Gilles Prison on 7 August. Her first recorded interrogation by Lieutenant

Bergan was on Sunday 8 August. Pinkhoff interpreted Bergan's German questions as well as asking his own in French. He then interpreted Edith's French responses to be written in German by Sergeant Neuhaus, the clerk and witness. Once her statement was taken, Pinkhoff translated it back to her in French before she signed it. Otto Mayer was also present for the interrogation.

Pinkhoff told Edith that they had all the information they needed, and the best way to save the others was to confess everything. Bergan later admitted that they tricked her by pretending to know more than they did. For example, they accused Edith of receiving 5,000 francs from Prince Reginald de Croy. Naively Edith responded, 'No, not 5,000, it was only 500.'

After this first slip, Edith realized their deceit. Four years later, Mayer gave evidence at Quien's trial and said that Edith answered evasively for the rest of the interview. But the statement that was written for her in German listed the names of those she had worked with, the numbers of men 'of military age' she accommodated at the training hospital, the names of those who had funded the operation, and the meeting points she used to link escapees with guides.

Edith signed the statement assuming Pinkhoff had translated it correctly for her from German. She was charged with 'conducting soldiers to the enemy'; these charges were outlined in the German Military Code and carried a death sentence. After her execution, the German propaganda machine tried to turn popular opinion against Edith by saying, falsely, that she was the only one to provide a signed statement. They accused her of betraying her fellow defendants, when in fact all thirty-five had signed statements written for them in German.

Her second interrogation on 18 August stressed 'of all the soldiers lodging with me, only two or three were wounded, and that only slightly'. This signed statement strongly suggests that Edith's evidence was being distorted, as many of the men that Edith cared for were badly injured. Edith's love of truth would not have allowed her to sign this false statement if she had known its correct translation. But this fact was crucial to the prosecution's case, as able-bodied soldiers who had been helped to escape could return to battle against the German army.

Edith's third statement was taken on 22 August, this time implicating the Countess de Belleville. By then Edith was a prisoner in St Gilles Prison. Her day began at 5 a.m. Breakfast of coffee and bread was brought to their cells at 7 a.m., then they had a visit from the prison sergeant at 8 a.m. Bizarrely he sold postcards and newspapers, took orders for the canteen, and delivered letters. Lunch was at midday: soup, meat, and potatoes with a glass of Faro, a cheap, light, sweet beer made locally. The last meal of the day was at 5 p.m.: coffee, bread, and cheese. Then lights out at 9 p.m. If the prisoner was sentenced to death, the light stayed on all night, with regular checks by patrolling prison guards.

Edith was allowed one concession. On Sundays her midday meal was supplied by the training hospital kitchen, brought to her by one of the staff, reminiscent of those days in Norfolk when Edith had been dispatched to share the family's Sunday lunch with villagers.

The cells were spartan, with a folding bed which doubled as a table in the day, a wooden chair, a small cupboard, a jug of water, and a metal bucket for waste. There were wooden floors and plain walls with no decoration apart from a crucifix.

Prisoners were allowed some exercise and fresh air, but when they were with other prisoners they had to wear a linen hood which covered their head and face, only showing their eyes.

On 23 August, Edith wrote to Elisabeth Wilkins: 'I have asked to see you but it may not be till after sentence, so do not try any more – just write all you want to know and I will reply on the first occasion.' She was anxious about the continuing work of the hospital but Grace and Pauline were her first concerns. She explained their finances:

> Miss Jemmett owes the Sch. about 420 frs – I send her 25 frs to be kept by you for immediate needs. Tell M Heger [one of the doctors at the training hospital] all about her professionally and ask him to do what he can for her – explain that it is since last year only she has been so ill and tell him I have done all in my power, as we cannot communicate with her father. I have been obliged to go on as you know – he will pay all expense on the first opportunity. I do hope he will allow her to stay as a patient – otherwise I cannot see what will become of her.

She added:

> Pauline's money is in the bank and she shall have it when I am again free. I send 25 frs also for her wants. Will you explain her case to M Heger and tell him that she has been with us over 2 years and is only 16, and that she is my godchild. Perhaps he will let her stay as she works well, and I am afraid greatly for her if she left.

Edith wrote optimistically. She answered a few other practical questions, then asked Elisabeth to send her a comb, notepaper, hankies, and two books: her prayer book and her copy of *The Imitation of Christ*.

'My dear old Jack!' was on her mind too. 'Please brush him sometimes and look after him.'

She wanted Elisabeth and the nurses to know 'I am quite well – more worried about the Sch. than my own fate. Tell the girls to be good and work well and be tidy' and added, 'Are all my things put away safely? with camphor? Don't buy anything for me, I do very well with what I have.'

And always concerned that her nurses should do well, she added the PS: 'Please see the nurses going for their exam for the 2nd time in October study regularly.'

Back in England on 23 August, news of Edith's arrest finally reached her family. Her brother-in-law Longworth Wainwright wrote to the foreign secretary asking for up-to-date information. All they had been told was that Edith was arrested on 5 August. Foreign secretary Sir Edward Grey then sent a telegram to the American ambassador in London and on 27 August, Brand Whitlock, the minister at the American consulate in Brussels, was contacted. Four days later, Whitlock started making enquiries of Baron von der Lancken, the German governor. When ten days passed without a response, Whitlock wrote again to the baron. His reply confirmed Edith Cavell had been arrested: 'She herself has admitted that she concealed in her house French and English soldiers, as well as Belgians of military age, all desirous of proceeding to the front...'

Edith was in solitary confinement and was not allowed visits from a defence lawyer, he added. Whitlock wrote to the British foreign secretary, updating them on Edith's arrest and admission, promising 'to keep this case in view and endeavour[ing] to see that a fair trial is given to Miss Cavell...'

The Foreign Office did nothing, claiming to be powerless. Their conclusion: 'Any representation from us will do her more harm than good.'

Without her prayer book for most of August, Edith would have relied on the familiar words of the Book of Common Prayer, which she had prayed daily for nearly half a century. Each day began and ended with words of Scripture, the Lord's Prayer, the Creed, and the Grace. Now more than ever Edith would have put her heart into the words: 'O Lord, make haste to help us.'

Her letters show that she used her time to tie up loose ends in her financial affairs and to think about her nurses and their new school, which she would never see in action. She wrote to the nurses on 14 September thanking them for the roses and chrysanthemums they had sent:

> Your delightful letter gave me great pleasure, and your lovely flowers have made my cell gay, the roses are still fresh, but the chrysanthemums did not like prison any more than I do – hence they did not live very long.
>
> I am happy to know that you are working well, that you are devoted to your patients and that you are happy in your services. It is necessary that you should study well, for some of you must shortly sit for your examinations and I will want you very much to succeed. The year's course will commence shortly, try to profit from it, and be punctual at lectures so that your

professor need not be kept waiting.

In everything one can learn new lessons of life, and if you were in my place you would realise how precious liberty is, and would certainly undertake never to abuse it.

To be a good nurse one must have lots of patience – here one learns to have that quality, I assure you.

The new school was nearly ready, and Jose was helping the nurses to move the furniture in on a handcart. She ended the letter:

It appears that the new school is advancing – I hope to see it again one of these days, as well as all of you.

Au revoir, be really good.

Your devoted Matron,

E. Cavell

Fellow prisoner Philippe Baucq was not proving to be such a compliant prisoner. Again his inquisitors used a trick to get his confession. On 15 September, Neels de Rhode was taken to Baucq's cell pretending to be a patriotic Belgian being bullied by the Germans. Baucq tried to cheer him up by telling de Rhode how he passed messages to fellow prisoners by tapping the heating pipes. He even explained some of his involvement in the resistance work. De Rhode was taken from the cell that afternoon. Baucq didn't see him again, but the evidence de Rhode passed on resulted in Baucq being moved to another cell, and was used at his trial.

The dossier of evidence against the resistance movement was stacking up. Bergan, Pinkhoff, and Mayer had amassed files on thirty-five members of the Belgian resistance movement. Edith knew that the trial was imminent. She asked Elisabeth to send her blue coat and skirt, a white muslin blouse, thick reindeer gloves, a grey fur stole, and six stamps. These were the civilian clothes she wore to the trial, rather than her nurse's uniform. The gloves were, perhaps, because she expected to be sent to an internment camp or German prison for the rest of the war.

On 3 October, seventeen of the nurses at the training hospital signed a letter written for them in flamboyant German to Baron von Bissing, the governor general in Belgium, asking for clemency for their matron. Rowland Ryder offered this translation:

> We the undersigned nurses of the Clinic situated
> at 32 rue de Bruxelles-Uccle, Brussels (formerly
> 149 rue de la Culture), humbly take the liberty, on
> consideration of your benevolent intentions towards
> the whole population, of approaching your Excellency
> in the hope of shortening the term of imprisonment
> of our former matron, Miss Cavell, who was arrested
> on 5.8.15, and, if it were in any way practicable, of
> procuring the suspension thereof. We would make
> known to your Excellency that Miss Cavell has
> superintended our Clinic for eight years, and has won
> by her self-sacrificing work lasting recognition in the
> service of charity from all her patients as well as her
> staff. Confident in the benevolent reception which

> your Excellency will recognize our sad position, and
> graciously set our minds at rest concerning the fate of
> our esteemed Matron. In this hope we beg to assure
> your Excellency of our lasting gratitude.

It made no difference.

Further down the chain of command, General von Sauberzweig was appointed military governor of Brussels, replacing a more lenient officer. Von Sauberzweig had a personal reason to hate the English. His son had been blinded in battle. He argued that one of the men who had escaped from Belgium to fight again could have been responsible. Von Sauberzweig appointed the military prosecutor for the trial, Dr Eduard Stoeber, who was notoriously ruthless and particularly harsh. The case against Edith Cavell and her fellow defendants was his first in Brussels. He wanted to make his mark.

The thirty-four who were accused alongside Edith included those who had sheltered the escaping soldiers, the guides, and the chemists who helped to provide photographs and identity papers. They were taken from St Gilles Prison to the impressive Senate Chamber on Thursday 7 October to face five judges. They had no opportunity to consult with their defence lawyers, who did not know the charges against the prisoners until they heard Stoeber's prosecution case in court. The proceedings were held in German, with some translation into French.

Sadi Kirschen had been appointed to defend Edith, but he had not talked with her before the trial and had to conduct the defence in German, not his first language. He noticed that Edith moved very quietly and had chosen civilian dress rather than her nurses' uniform for her court appearance. Edith was the first to be questioned, and answered Stoeber's questions calmly and clearly in fluent French, though with her distinctive English accent. When asked why she had been involved, she explained: 'I was sent to begin with, two Englishmen who were in danger of death…'

She believed that they would be shot, but explained, 'My preoccupation has not been to aid the enemy but to help men who applied to me to reach the frontier; once across the frontier, they were free.'

She admitted sending 'about 200' men to the frontier. Rowland Ryder later calculated that it was likely to have been at least 1,000 men. But there was little time for details. The entire prosecution cross-examination of Edith was just a dozen questions and answers, reported by Sadi Kirchen and recorded by Rowland Ryder as follows:

Stoeber

From November 1914 to July 1915 you have lodged French and English soldiers, including a colonel, all in civilian clothes; you have helped Belgians, French and English of military age, in furnishing them with the means of going to the front, notably in receiving them at your nursing home and in giving them money?

Edith Cavell

Yes.

Stoeber

With whom were you concerned in committing these acts?

Edith Cavell

With M. Capiau, Mlle Martin (Mlle Thuliez), MM Derveau and Libiez.

Stoeber

Who was the head, the originator of the organization?

Edith Cavell

There wasn't a head of the organization.

Stoeber

Wasn't it the Prince de Croy?

Edith Cavell

No. The Prince de Croy confined himself to sending men to whom he had given a little money.

Stoeber

Why have you committed these acts?

Edith Cavell

I was sent, to begin with, two Englishmen who were in danger of death; one was wounded.

[Stoeber took objection to this comment and said that under German military law this was out of the question, but Edith repeated that she believed they would have been shot.]

Stoeber

Once these people crossed the frontier did they send you news to that effect?

Edith Cavell

Four or five only did so.

[This was a seriously incriminating fact as it meant that soldiers had escaped and could return to the front line in the war against Germany.]

Stoeber

Baucq and Fromage are the same person?

Edith Cavell

Yes.

Stoeber

What was Baucq's role?

Edith Cavell

I knew him very little. I only met him once, and I don't know what his role was.

Stoeber

Do you maintain what you said at the interrogation concerning the people with whom you worked with a view to recruiting, that is to say Prince Reginald de Croy, Baucq, Séverin, Capiau, Libiez, Derveau, Mlle Thuliez and Mme Ada Bodart?

Edith Cavell

Yes.

Stoeber

Do you realize that in thus recruiting men it would be to the disadvantage of Germany and to the advantage of the enemy?

Edith Cavell

My preoccupation has not been to aid the enemy but to help the men who applied to me reach the frontier; once across the frontier, they were free.

Stoeber

How many people have you thus sent to the frontier?

Edith Cavell

About two hundred.

Then proceedings moved on to the next defendant, Louise Thuliez. Her motive: 'Because I am French.'

Philippe Baucq infuriated Stoeber when he confirmed his name and added, 'Yes, and a good patriot.' Patriotism was not a sufficient defence. The patriotism theme continued when Ada Bodart was asked if she was a patriot. She replied that patriotism was not a fault.

It took just two and a half hours to question the twelve principal defendants. They then stopped for lunch and Louise Thuliez took the opportunity to whisper to Edith, asking her how she thought the trial was going. 'I think that Baucq, Capiau, you and I stand a bad chance,' she replied, 'but what does it matter so long as we are not shot.'

From two o'clock onwards, the remaining twenty-three prisoners were cross-examined. Among them was fourteen-year-old Philippe Bodart, who had been arrested at Baucq's house. Philippe was reminded that it was a sin for a Christian not to speak the truth, and the sentence for perjury was ten years hard labour. Then he was asked if Baucq had delivered parcels of *La Libre Belgique* to his mother's house and also, if Baucq had told him he was tracing out the route for escaping soldiers to take to the frontier. Baucq jumped up at this point to explain that the boy would not have understood precisely what had been said, as he spoke English at home. His objection was ignored and Philippe's reply incriminated his own mother. He was allowed to hug her to say goodbye before leaving the court. It was now 7 p.m. and the court adjourned for the day.

The next day, Friday 8 October, proceedings resumed at 8 a.m. Stoeber's prosecution speech lasted three and a half hours. There was no break for lunch and no translation until the final stage, when an interpreter read the sentences that Stoeber was demanding: the death sentence for Philippe Baucq, Louise Thuliez, Edith Cavell and six others, with hard labour varying from five to ten years for the rest. Edith remained unperturbed and calm as the interpreter listed Stoeber's demands.

Sadi Kirschen opened the defence for Edith Cavell and eight others. When invited to make her own defence statement, Edith said simply, 'I have nothing to add' and sat down. But at the end of the afternoon, Princess Marie de Croy asked permission to speak.

> Everyone must be prepared to take full responsibility for their acts and I want to bear full responsibility for mine. It has been said that Miss Cavell was at the head of a conspiracy: that she organised the escape of British and the recruitment of French and Belgians. It is not true. She was forced into it by my brother and me. It was we who at the beginning sheltered and hid these men. When she told us she could lodge no more, that her

institution would be endangered if we sent more to her,
we still took her others, and so did our confederates …
it is not on her, but on us, on my brother and me, that
the greater part of the responsibility for these acts lies. I
am ready to pay the penalty…

The princess had passed a message on a page torn from her
prayer book to her defence lawyer before the trial, asking him
to give her a sign when she entered the court to show that her
brother had escaped. She did not want to put him in danger.
She was ready to take the blame herself. But her selfless bid was
ignored. The court rose at 4 p.m., and the defendants were told
they would hear their sentences later in the prison.

Edith and Jeanne de Belleville travelled back to St Gilles in
the same prison van. Edith asked the guard if it was true that
women were no longer being condemned to death. His positive
response gave them some hope. But she hoped in vain.

The judges considered their verdict in secret on Saturday 9
October. Their official report, recorded in translation by A. E.
Clark-Kennedy, stated:

The Court is of the opinion, partly on the strength
of the prisoners' own statements and partly on the
assertions of their fellow prisoners, that Croy, Baucq,
Thuliez, Cavell, Belleville and Séverin were the chief
organizers of two seditious groups, one in northern
France and one in the Borinage, which helped English
and French fugitive soldiers and French and Belgians
of military age to escape into Holland whence they
might join the Allied armies. The chateau at Bellignies

was the principal meeting place on the way to Holland via Brussels. This had been put at the disposal of the organization by the Prince de Croy, his sister giving hospitality to the men and taking photographs of them in order to enable Capiau and Derveau to fake identity papers in which British and French soldiers were stated to be of Belgian nationality. The men were then brought to Brussels and hidden in different places by Cavell until they could be taken over the frontier by guides hired for this work. In this way Cavell had made it possible for some two hundred and fifty men to reach Holland. Her chief assistant was Baucq. Six of these men let those who had helped them know that they had arrived in England or France. Further, in the opinion of this Court most of the prisoners were aware that they were conveying fugitive soldiers and men of military age to the enemy. It was their deliberate intention to supply reinforcements to the hostile powers to the detriment of our own German troops.

On Monday 11 October, the prisoners were taken from their cells to the central hall of the prison. Stoeber arrived, together with the German chaplains and the prison governor. He then read the sentences:

Philippe Baucq	Death
Louise Thuliez	Death
Edith Cavell	Death
Louise Severin	Death
Jeanne de Belleville	Death

Edith was leaning against a wall when one of her fellow prisoners said, 'Make an appeal for mercy.' 'It is useless,' she replied. 'I am English and they want my life.'

Pastor Le Seur, the German Lutheran chaplain, took Edith into a side room to talk privately. 'How long will they give me?' she asked him. 'Unfortunately only until morning,' he replied. He then offered to contact Revd Stirling Gahan, to bring her Holy Communion.

Alone in her cell, Edith turned to prayer, to reading *The Imitation of Christ* and to writing her last letters.

To her nurses she wrote in French:

> This is a sad moment for me as I write to say good-bye. It reminds me that on the 17th September I had been running the school for eight years.
>
> I was so happy to be called to help in the organization of the work which our Committee had just founded. On the 1st October 1907 there were only four young pupils, whereas now you are many – fifty or sixty in all I believe, including those who have obtained their certificates and are about to leave the School …

She recalled some of their achievements, and added:

> … it is a good thing sometimes to stop and look back upon the path we have travelled to take stock of our progress and the mistakes we have made. To my sorrow I have not always been able to talk to you each privately. You know that I had my share of burdens. But I hope that you will not forget our evening chats …

She reminded them:

> I told you that devotion would bring you true happiness
> and the thought that, before God and in your own eyes,
> you have done your duty well and with a good heart,
> will sustain you in trouble and face to face with death.

Edith's own devotion to duty was, no doubt, sustaining her as she faced her own death. Mindful of her own failings she added, 'If any of you has a grievance against me, I beg you to forgive me; I have perhaps been unjust sometimes, but I have loved you much more than you think.'

She also wrote a personal note to Sister Elisabeth Wilkins, asking her to 'take charge of my will':

> My dear Sister,
>
> Mr Gahan will give you twenty francs from me to pay
> my little debts. Miss J. owes me (she will remember)
> 100 francs. Take it to buy a clock for the entrance hall.
> It was given me by Mr Mayer. [Was this odd reference
> to one of her inquisitors a warning for Elisabeth?]
>
> At the end of the daily account book you will see the
> Red Cross accounts. Money spent out of school funds
> but not entered should be covered by the two cheques I
> have told you of and which are not entered either.
>
> I am asking you to take charge of my will and a few
> things for me.
>
> You have been very kind my dear, and I thank you
> and the nurses for all you have done for me in the last
> ten weeks. My love to you all, I am not afraid but quite
> happy.

Her letter to Grace was more personal, like a mother to a daughter:

> My dear Girl,
>
> How shall I write to you this last day? Standing where I stand now, the world looks very far away. I worried about you a great deal at first, but I know God will do for you abundantly above all that I can ask or think, and He loves you so much better than I …

Edith urged Grace to live:

> … as I would have you live. Nothing matters when one comes to the last hour but a clear conscience, and life looks so wasted and full of wrong-doing and things left undone.
>
> You have helped me often, my dear, and in ways you little dreamed of, and I have remembered our happy holidays with Mother and many small pleasures. I want you to go to England at once now and ask – to be put where you can be cured [she had become addicted to morphine after treatment for an illness]. Don't mind how hard it is, do it for my sake, and try and find something useful to do, something to make you forget yourself while making others happy.

Finding something useful to do, forgetting herself while making others happy, had been one of Edith's principles for life.

Urging Grace to make her own peace with God, she added:

> If God permits, I shall watch over you and wait for you
> on the other side. Be sure to get ready for then. I want
> you to know that I am neither afraid nor unhappy, but
> quite ready to give my life for England.

The letter ends:

> I am sending you my wrist watch by Mr Gahan because
> it was always with me and I know you will like to wear
> it. I shall pray to God at the last that He will keep you
> in His tender care. Forgive me that I have been severe
> sometimes; it has been a great grief to me to remember
> it. I think I was too anxious about you last year and
> that is why. I am sure you will forget it now and only
> remember that I loved you and love you still.

Although Edith also wrote a final letter to her mother, it was never delivered and its contents remain unknown. Having asked forgiveness of those closest to her, Edith wrote her own epitaph in her copy of *The Imitation of Christ*.

> Arrested 5 August 1915
> Brussels Prison de St Gilles 7 Aug 1915
> Court martialled 7 Oct 1915
>   "   "   8 " "
> Condemned to death 8 Oct
> in the Salle des deputés at 10.30 a.m. with 7 others.
> (The accused numbered in all 70 of whom 34 were
> present on these 2 dates.)
> Died 7 a.m. on Oct 12th 1915
> E. Cavell
>
> With love to E. D. Cavell.

She left the book to cousin Eddy Cavell.

The Imitation of Christ, which she so valued, is written as a conversation between 'the Disciple' – the follower of Jesus, and the 'Beloved' – God himself. Edith marked sixty different passages in her copy of the book and dated some of them, giving an insight into her thoughts. In particular she highlighted two chapters while imprisoned during October 1915. In the chapter entitled: 'How we ought to call upon God, and to bless Him, when Tribulation is upon us', she marked this prayer:

> Grant me patience, O Lord, even now in this
> emergency.
> Help me, my God, and then I will not fear, how
> grievously soever I be afflicted.
> And now amidst these my troubles what shall I say?
> Lord, thy will be done; I have well deserved to be
> afflicted and weighed down.
> Therefore I ought to bear it; and O that I may bear it
> with patience, until the tempest pass over, and all be
> well again, or even better!

She also marked 'St Gilles Oct 1915' at the start of the chapter 'Of craving the Divine Aid, and Confidence of recovering Grace' which is a response from God:

> I am the Lord, that giveth strength in the day of
> tribulation.
> Come thou unto Me, when it is not well with thee …
> Gather strength again in the light of My mercies; for
> I am at hand (saith the Lord) to repair all, not only

entirely, but also abundantly and in most plentiful measure.

Is there anything hard to Me? or shall I be like one that saith and doeth not?

Where is thy faith? stand firmly and with perseverance; take courage and be patient; comfort will come to thee in due time …

Let not therefore thy heart be troubled, neither let it fear.

Trust in Me, and put thy confidence in My mercy. When thou thinkest thyself farthest off from Me, oftentimes I am nearest unto thee.

When thou countest almost all to be lost, then oftentimes the greatest gain of reward is close at hand …

Think not thyself wholly left, although for a time I have sent thee some tribulation, or have even withdrawn thy desired comfort; for this is the way to the Kingdom of Heaven …

'As the Father hath loved Me, I also love you,' said I unto My beloved disciples; whom certainly I sent not out to temporal joys, but to great conflicts; not to honours, but to contempts; not to idleness, but to labours; not to rest, but to bring forth much fruit with patience. Remember thou these words …

On Saturday 9 October 1915, after the trial, perhaps still hoping for freedom, she had underlined this prayer drawn from Psalm 31: 'Display Thy wonderful works, I beseech Thee, and let Thy right hand be glorified; for there is no other hope, or refuge for me, save in Thee, O Lord my God.'

On Sunday 10 October, she had highlighted chapter 35 – 'That there is no Security from Temptation in this Life'. The chapter is written as if by God to his followers:

> ... thou art never secure in this life, but, as long as thou livest, thou shalt always need spiritual armour.
>
> Thou dwellest among enemies, and art assaulted on the right hand and on the left.
>
> If therefore thou defend not thyself on every side with the shield of patience, thou wilt not be long without a wound.
>
> Moreover, if thou set not thy heart fixedly on Me, with a sincere wish to suffer all things for Me, thou wilt not be able to bear the heat of this combat ...
>
> ... If thou seek rest in this life, how wilt thou then attain to the everlasting rest?
>
> Dispose not thyself for much rest, but for great patience.
>
> Seek true peace, not in earth, but in Heaven; not in men, nor in any other creature, but in God alone.
>
> For the love of God thou oughtest cheerfully to undergo all things, that is to say, all labour and pain, temptation, vexation, anxiety, necessity, infirmity, injury, obloquy, reproof, humiliation, confusion, correction, and scorn.
>
> These help to virtue; these are the trial of a Novice in Christ; these frame the Heavenly Crown.
>
> I will give you an everlasting reward for a short labour, and infinite glory for transitory confusion ...

She particularly highlighted the words: 'I will be with thee in every tribulation.'

For Edith, these words were a reminder of the eternal rest and peace awaiting those who follow Christ.

On Monday 11 October 1915, she marked several passages in the section on the 'Comfort of Devout Communion':

> I am racked with grief of heart, I am burdened with
> sins, I am troubled with temptations, I am entangled
> and oppressed with many evil passions; and there is
> none to help me, none to deliver me and save me, but
> Thou O Lord God my Saviour, to whom I commit
> myself and all that is mine, that Thou mayest keep
> watch over me, and bring me safe to everlasting.

The final passage Edith marked in the book focuses on the forgiveness God promises. It is a call to repent and follow Jesus:

> Then with full resignation and with thy entire will, offer
> up thyself to the honour of My Name, on the altar of thy
> heart a perpetual whole burnt offering even thy body
> and soul, faithfully committing them unto Me ...
>
> And when a man shall have done what lieth in him,
> and shall be truly penitent, how often soever he shall
> come to Me for pardon and grace, 'as I live' saith the
> Lord, ... 'I will not remember his sins any more, but they
> shall all be forgiven him'.

When Revd Stirling Gahan arrived to share Holy Communion with her on that last evening, she had prepared her heart to meet her Maker. She was grateful for the ten weeks of quiet after such a busy life. She told him:

> I have no fear nor shrinking … I have seen death so
> often that it is not strange or fearful to me … life has
> always been hurried and full of difficulty. This time of
> rest has been a great mercy. Everyone here has been
> very kind. This I would say, standing as I do in view
> of God and Eternity, I realize that patriotism is not
> enough. I must have no hatred or bitterness towards
> anyone.

She knew that the patriotism her fellow prisoners had used in their defence was not enough to enable her to stand in God's presence. Just as she had said daily, in repeating the Lord's Prayer morning and evening, 'forgive us our trespasses, As we forgive them that trespass against us' she knew that she couldn't hold on to hatred or bitterness. She needed to forgive others, just as she had been forgiven.

After they had shared communion, they said together the words of the hymn 'Abide With Me', and Edith asked Revd Gahan about heaven. He recalled:

> I told her the story of the thief on the cross, with the
> Saviour's assuring words 'today shalt thou be with me
> in paradise'. Jesus was almighty to forgive and to save,
> and to admit all his pardoned ones into his Blessed
> Presence and Rest. This covered all the need and ended
> all anxiety.

When Revd Gahan said, 'We shall always remember you as a heroine and a martyr,' she replied, 'Don't think of me like that, think of me only as a nurse who tried to do her duty.'

As he left her cell, she took his hand and said with confidence in her eternal future, 'We shall meet again.'

Her last glimpse of life on the earth would be the gloomy mists of an autumn dawn in Belgium. Her expectation was that in the 'twinkling of an eye' (1 Corinthians 15:52), she would be in the presence of Jesus.

Heaven's morning breaks, and earth's vain shadows flee;
In life, in death, O Lord, abide with me.

CHAPTER 12

A LEGACY OF HOPE

I SHALL THINK OF YOU TO THE LAST, AND YOU MAY BE SURE WE
SHALL DO OUR DUTY HERE AND DIE AS WOMEN OF OUR RACE
SHOULD DIE.

(Edith Cavell, in a letter left for her mother and family)

Before dawn on 12 October, the prison guard opened her cell
door to find Edith kneeling, praying by her bed. Overnight
there had been a flurry of activity as the nurses and staff from
the American consulate had tried in vain to gain a reprieve for
Edith. She and Philippe Baucq were to be executed without
delay. The other death sentences had been deferred.

The German Lutheran priest, Pastor Paul Le Seur,
accompanied Edith from the prison to the Tir National, the
shooting range where 250 soldiers were waiting. On the way,
the car passed Sister Elisabeth Wilkins who had been standing
in the rain for two hours with some of the nurses to catch a
glimpse of their matron. Elisabeth said Edith was wearing her
blue uniform, sitting bolt upright between two German guards.

Philippe Baucq was accompanied to his execution by the
Catholic priest. In his last letter to his wife, Baucq said:

> I die for my country, without regretting what I have
> done; I die as a Christian. My greatest suffering is to
> leave you, my dear wife, my dear children, for I have
> always loved you and will love you until my last breath.
> God ... has called me, and I submit as a Christian, to his
> decision ... later we will meet again in heaven ...

Before the sentences were read, Baucq called out, 'Comrades, in the presence of death we are all comrades.' But he was stopped from saying more by the prosecutor Dr Stoeber. The sentences were read in German and French, then the clergymen were allowed a few final minutes with the prisoners.

Pastor Le Seur took Edith's hand and said the words of the Grace: 'The Grace of our Lord Jesus Christ, and the love of God and the fellowship of the Holy Ghost be with us all evermore. Amen.'

Her last words were: 'Ask Mr Gahan to tell my loved ones that my soul I believe is safe, and that I am glad to die for my country.'

The soldier who tied her blindfold said her eyes were full of tears.

When Philippe Baucq was also ready, the command was given to the waiting marksmen. His last words were *'Vive la Belgique.'* Two groups of eight men fired simultaneously from a distance of six paces. Edith died instantly with one shot to her forehead and three through her chest. The chief medical officer certified her death, closed her eyes, and placed her body in a coffin, which was lowered into a waiting grave.

The news of Edith Cavell's death reached England four days later. A War Office official was told to telephone Mrs Cavell to break the news to her. In the event he phoned the wrong Mrs Cavell to say 'Your daughter in Brussels has been shot by the Germans'. The Mrs Cavell he had reached was a relative of Edith's, who told the insensitive War Office official, 'When you get in touch with the right Mrs Cavell you won't put it quite like that, will you? She's a very old lady and she isn't very well.'

A few press reports appeared on Saturday 16 October, and from Monday 18 October British newspapers were full of eulogies and calls for vengeance. On 21 October, the Bishop of London, preaching at St Martin-in-the-Fields, commented that Britain no longer needed a recruitment campaign. Edith's execution was enough. 'Who will avenge Nurse Cavell?' became a recruiting slogan. The number of volunteers joining up had been around 6,000 a week at that point in the war. In the week ending 27 October 1915, they jumped to 11,423, with well over 10,000 volunteering each week through to the end of November.

As reports appeared in newspapers around the world, Edith's story began to shake America out of its neutral stance on the war. The British Prime Minister, Lord Asquith, told the House of Commons, 'She has taught the bravest man among us the supreme lesson of courage.'

Prince Reginald de Croy had escaped to London before the trial, and he wrote to Mrs Cavell on 18 October.

> I have learned with deep sorrow the terrible news from Brussels. It was my privilege to know and to visit your daughter often in the latter months. The great and noble work which she undertook with such admirable courage and patriotism has been deeply appreciated

by all who were associated with her; she was ever ready to come to the assistance of those who were suffering through the war. The crime for which she was convicted was Pity and Humanity which in the eyes of the Germans was a crime worthy of death.

As well as conveying his condolences, the prince's letter carried a note of urgency.

May I beg you however to refuse to give any particulars concerning her work on behalf of the soldiers, as anything published now endangers the lives of the many others who are condemned but still unexecuted so far as we know, among whom is my own sister.

Hundreds of letters, with their black mourning edge, were soon arriving at Mrs Cavell's house. The Bishop of Norwich, who visited her at home, said the 81-year-old was quite bewildered by it all. 'Her little room was strewn with letters and telegrams.'

The Belgian government and the French ambassador sent their condolences, and Queen Alexandra's chaplain wrote to Mrs Cavell on 18 October from the rectory at Sandringham assuring her of the queen's prayers.

I am commanded by Her Majesty Queen Alexandra to write and say how deeply Her Majesty feels for you in the sad and tragic loss of your daughter … always remember that she never failed England in her time of need … The name of Miss Cavell will be held in highest honour and respect …

A memorial service was held for Edith at St Paul's Cathedral on 29 October 1915. It began with the hymn 'Abide With Me', and included Paul's triumphant declaration:

> Behold, I shew you a mystery; We shall not all sleep, but we shall all be changed, In a moment, in the twinkling of an eye, at the last trump: for the trumpet shall sound, and the dead shall be raised incorruptible, and we shall be changed. (1 Corinthians 15: 51–52, KJV)

The Bishop of Durham, Handley Dunelm, who had lost his own 22-year-old daughter a few years earlier, wrote to Mrs Cavell on 25 October. As well as offering his sympathy, he wrote to encourage her in her faith, reminding her that 'Your Lord, and the Lord and exemplar of your daughter ... is with you, and that in His presence of all faithful love you will find rest "until the Day breaks".'

Referring to Jesus' second coming, he added, 'It may not be very long now before His Coming puts an end to all the shadows from His people, and "abolishes death" and the grave forever.'

His letter reflects the warning in Mark's Gospel that the end of time would be preceded by 'wars and rumours of wars ... Nation will rise against nation, and kingdom against kingdom. There will be earthquakes in various places, and famines ...' (Mark 13:7–8).

While the horror of the First World War prompted many to question whether God existed, many others saw it as a fulfilment of biblical prophecy.

The bishop concluded that letter, 'And what glory is mingled with your grief! That holy heroism of faith, courage, love & peace will never be forgotten.'

It was the first in a long correspondence between the Bishop of Durham and Mrs Cavell as he sought to bring her comfort, reminding her: 'He is with you. And His heart knows all about grief.'

He visited Mrs Cavell the following summer and prayed with her. Later, he wrote:

> I saw in your own spirit of calm submission, amidst your great sorrow ... some of the secret of Miss Cavell's blessed life and its closing victory. She saw, all her life, in her Mother, the deep & tranquil power of the Spirit of our blessed Lord & Saviour ... May you be spared some years to witness to Christ's blessed peace, as you did to me. It will be a little minute from the endless life awaiting you with Edith & with her Father, in the presence of the Lord.

Evidently the bishop had taken time to listen to Mrs Cavell's story and to hear how she had found a measure of peace and comfort from knowing that her daughter shared her faith in Jesus. He wrote again just before the first anniversary of Edith's execution, proposing that a 'home of rest for nurses' be opened in Edith's memory. It was one of many institutions opened around the world, bearing Edith Cavell's name.

> Innumerable people all over the world will be thinking of you and prayers untold will go up for you as October 12th draws on. But oh! Your mother's heart will need deeper

comfort than that, as you see, with the sight of your soul, your little child, your noble gifted daughter, your dear young probationer nurse, and then her later splendid service for the suffering in her own way, and then in the dark passage at the end into the boundless light. I just commend you with my whole heart to your once suffering, heartbroken Saviour, who now lives to bless you, and with whom your Edith lives, all light and love.

The bishop also wrote to her when he saw a picture of Edith above a wounded soldier's bed – 'Oh how she lives on earth in grateful memory', he added.

On the second anniversary of Edith's death, he wrote again: 'I pray that the eternal Friend may daily and hourly breathe into your soul His "everlasting" comfort and good hope through grace.'

Mrs Cavell ended her days living with Edith's sister Lilian and her husband, Longworth Wainwright. She died on 17 June 1918, and was buried next to her husband in the graveyard at Swardeston.

The war ended a few months later, and plans were made to bring Edith's body back to England. Jack, Edith's dog, was given a new home with Princess Marie at Bellignies. The princess was court martialled and imprisoned again in the Second World War for sheltering fugitives, but lived into her nineties. Louise Thuliez went back to teaching, but also resumed her resistance activities in the Second World War, living for more than fifty years after she had been condemned to death with Edith. Elisabeth Wilkins returned to England, where she became matron of a cottage hospital in Somerset. The new school opened and was named the *Insitut Edith Cavell – Marie Depage* in memory of the two women who had played such a significant role in its history.

Edith's body was exhumed on 13 March 1919. Her features were still recognizable, and a post-mortem confirmed that she had been killed by four bullets. Revd Gahan conducted a service at the Gare du Nord in Brussels before her body was taken back to Britain. The Belgian army guarded Edith's coffin, which was laid on a gun carriage for the journey from Brussels to Ostend, where the Royal Navy took over. Florence Cavell and Lilian Wainwright travelled with their sister's remains as they were escorted on the journey home by troops, nurses, and women from the First Aid Nursing Yeomanry. At Dover, the church bells were muffled for a peal of 5,040 changes lasting three hours. On the train journey from Dover to London, country stations were full of men, women, and children, gathered to pay their respects.

The first part of Edith's funeral service was held in Westminster Abbey. Edith would never have imagined that there could have been any fulfilment of her ambition to be buried in Westminster Abbey, which she had mentioned in the childish game played so many years before. The readings in the abbey included Revelation 21:1–7, the apostle John's vision of heaven, the source of John Bunyan's description in *The Pilgrim's Progress*:

> ... 'a new heaven and a new earth' ... the Holy City, the new Jerusalem, coming down out of heaven from God, prepared as a bride beautifully dressed for her husband. ... 'He will wipe every tear from their eyes. There will

be no more death' or mourning or crying or pain, for
the old order of things has passed away.'

He who was seated on the throne said, 'I am making
everything new!' … ' … I am the Alpha and the Omega,
the Beginning and the End. To the thirsty I will give
water without cost from the spring of the water of life.
Those who are victorious will inherit all this, and I will
be their God and they will be my children.'

The final stage of the journey was by train from London's
Liverpool Street station to Norwich and then on to Norwich
Cathedral. The service included words from 1 John 3:16,
emphasizing Edith's sacrificial love, following in the steps
of Jesus: 'This is how we know what love is: Jesus Christ laid
down his life for us. And we ought to lay down our lives for our
brothers and sisters.

Jack Cavell, Edith's brother, and cousin Eddy joined the
mourners at the cathedral. Sergeant Jesse Tunmore, who had
spent Christmas 1914 at the training hospital, was among the
last group of pall-bearers to carry the coffin from the cathedral
to its final resting place in the cathedral grounds.

Around the world, many remember her patriotism. But for
Edith, patriotism was not enough. Many saw her as a hero and a
martyr. Edith asked to be remembered '… only as a nurse who
tried to do her duty'.

As the Bishop of Durham said, she should never be
forgotten, for her faith in Jesus, courage in the face of death,
love expressed in practical, selfless service to friend and foe
alike, and her peace flowing from her confidence that because
of Jesus, death need not be the end.

RESOURCES

à Kempis, Thomas, *Of the Imitation of Christ – the 'Edith Cavell' edition*, Oxford: Oxford University Press, undated.

Boston, Noel, *The Dutiful Edith Cavell*, Norwich Cathedral, undated, circa 1971.

Bunyan, John, *The Pilgrim's Progress*. Accessed in June 2015 at http://www.gutenberg.org/files/131/131-h/131-h.htm

Clark-Kennedy, A. E., *Edith Cavell: Pioneer and Patriot*, London: Faber & Faber, 1965.

Daunton, Claire (ed.), *Edith Cavell: Her Life and Her Art*, Royal London Hospital Archives and Museum, 1990.

Evans, Jonathan, *Edith Cavell*, Royal London Hospital Museum, 2008.

Gahan, Revd H. Stirling, *The Execution of Edith Cavell* in *Records of the Great War*, Vol. III, ed. Charles F. Horne, National Alumni, 1923. Accessed in June 2015 at http://www.firstworldwar.com/source/cavell_gahan.htm

Harford, John Battersby and Frederick Charles Macdonald, *Handley Carr Glyn Moule, Bishop of Durham: a biography*, London: Hodder & Stoughton, 1922. Accessed in June 2015 http://archive.org/stream/handleycarrglynm00harf/handleycarrglynm00harf_djvu.txt

Hoehling, A. A., *Edith Cavell*, London: Cassell, 1958.

Imperial War Museum, *The First World War Papers of Edith Cavell*, on microfiche. Accessed in November 2014.

Judson, Helen, *Edith Cavell*, London, Macmillan, 1941.

Miller, Nick, *Edith Cavell – A Forgotten Heroine*, Cambridge: Grove Books, 2014.

Mortimer, Favell Lee, *The Peep of Day*, New York: Thomas Y. Crowell & Co, circa 1845.

Moyse, Cordelia, *A History of the Mothers' Union*, Woodbridge: Boydell Press, 2009.

Nightingale, Florence, 'Introductory notes on lying-in institutions' quoted in *Florence Nightingale (1820–1910): maternal mortality and the training of midwives* by Peter M. Dunn in the Archives of Disease in Childhood 1996; 74: F219-F220. Accessed in June 2015 at http://europepmc.org/backend/ptpmcrender.fcgi?accid=PMC2528337&blobtype=pdf

Peachment, Brian, *Ready to Die: Story of Edith Cavell*, Birmingham, AL: Religious Education Press, 1980.

Protheroe, Ernest, *A Noble Woman: The Life-Story of Edith Cavell*, London: Epworth Press, 1916. Republished in Fairford by the Echo Library, 2011.

Royal London Hospital Archives and Museum, London Hospital, 'A form of prayer to be read morning and evening, daily in every ward'.

Ryder, Rowland, *Edith Cavell*, London: Hamish Hamilton, 1975.

Souhami, Diana, *Edith Cavell*, London: Quercus, 2010.

Upjohn, Sheila, *Edith Cavell – The Story of a Norfolk Nurse*, Norwich Cathedral Publications, 2000.

White, William, *History, Gazetteer, and Directory of Norfolk 1883*.

Accessed in June 2015 at http://www.origins.org.uk/genuki/ NFK/places/s/swardeston/

The Daily Service-Book of the Church of England including the Book of Common Prayer, Oxford University Press, undated, circa 1911.

Census records 1841, 1851, 1861, 1871, 1881, 1891, 1901, 1911. Accessed via http://www.ancestry.co.uk

Hymns Ancient and Modern, 1874, 1896 and 1904 www.hymnary. org. Accessed in June 2015.

The archives and links from http://www.edithcavell.org.uk administered by Nick Miller. Accessed in June 2015.

Several of the sources used in this book are handwritten letters stored on microfiche in the Imperial War Museum in London, or recollections and records of conversations which took place in English, French, or German. I am grateful to the biographers who wrote in the decades closer to Edith's death and who transcribed and translated letters and interviews while they were still fully legible. I have compared the various sources to give as true a picture of Edith's life as I can, 100 years after her death.